luxury knits

luxury knits

Simple and stylish projects
for the most desirable knitwear

Amanda Griffiths

A QUARTO BOOK

First edition for the United States, Canada,
and its territories and possessions by
Barron's Educational Series, Inc. 2005.

All inquiries should be addressed to:
Barron's Educational Series, Inc.
250 Wireless Boulevard
Hauppauge, NY 11788
www.barronseduc.com

ISBN-13: 978-0-7641-5823-0

ISBN-10: 0-7641-5823-6

Library of Congress Catalog Card No.:
2004107403

QUAR.LKN

Conceived, designed, and produced by
Quarto Publishing plc
The Old Brewery
6 Blundell Street
London N7 9BH

Pattern writer Eva Yates
Project editor Jo Fisher
Art editor Anna Knight
Designer Jo Ridgeway
Illustrator Jennie Dooge
Assistant art director Penny Cobb
Photographer Jeff Cottenden
Knitters Gill Everett and her team
Copy editor Pauline Hornsby
Pattern checker Gill Everett
Proofreader Lydia Darbyshire
Indexer Diana LeCore

Art director Moira Clinch
Publisher Paul Carslake

Color separation by PICA Digital, Singapore
Printed by SNP Leefung Printers Limited,
China

9 8 7 6 5 4 3 2 1

contents

introduction

Knitting is far more than a relaxing way to spend spare time. It is a sensory experience of touch, feel, and color; a chance to create beautiful things and experience the pleasure of working with wonderful tactile yarns in lovely colors.

To knit something, whether it be for yourself or a loved one, involves an investment in time and is a unique personal statement that can evoke memories, mark an event, or be a special gift that is treasured and coveted for many years to come.

Luxury Knits is a collection of simple but stylish projects that use sumptuous yarns and fibers to create beautiful knitwear and accessory items. It includes twenty-two designs that incorporate everything from easy-knit scarves and drawstring bags to intricate lace sweaters.

The book is split into four sections, allowing the choice of creating exquisite gifts and accessories, luxury garments for summer or winter, or special day-to-evening pieces. All the designs have a timeless appeal, and the luxury fibers used make for extra special knitted items.

luxury yarns

Yarns are a wonderful source of inspiration. Color, texture, touch, and weight make the process of knitting the most pleasurable experience. Luxury fibers make for extra special pieces.

It is possible to spend hours indulging your senses, choosing from the most vivid colors to the palest hues, from the finest whisper-light yarns to the coziest yarns available.

types of yarns

Every yarn has its own unique characteristics and can be composed of a variety of fibers that make it so special.

Fibers are divided into two main types, natural and synthetic (manmade). Natural fibers are divided into two further categories: animal fibers—wool, cashmere, angora, silk; and vegetable fibers— cotton, linen, and hemp. Yarns of a natural origin are generally considered the more luxurious, although it is now quite common for natural yarns to have a small percentage of a synthetic fiber blended with them to create an unusual texture or quality, or to alter the characteristics, such as reducing the weight.

Wool

Wool is spun from the shorn fleece of sheep and is the fiber most commonly associated with knitting. Wool is a very versatile fiber as it blends well with other fibers and can be spun in a number of ways to affect the weight and quality of the yarn. It is often spun with a smooth appearance, which is good for showing stitch detail. Extra fine merino wool is generally regarded as the most luxurious and refined wool quality with which to work.

Cashmere

Cashmere is spun from the underhair of a particular Asian goat. It is associated with the ultimate in luxury as it is wonderfully soft to touch and beautiful to wear next to the skin. The price can often be quite prohibitive, but cashmere is now available blended with other fibers, making it more affordable while retaining the same fantastic qualities.

Angora

Like cashmere, angora (spun from angora rabbit fur) has a very luxurious, soft feel. It is often blended with other fibers but can still shed the hairs from the rabbit fur.

Silk

Silk fiber is produced by caterpillars as they form cocoons. Silk is available in two qualities: wild, which produces a coarse thread, and cultivated, which produces a finer thread. Both are expensive, and silk has a reputation for being extremely beautiful and luxurious. It is often blended with other fibers to make it more versatile, and can be spun to either a smooth yarn or a slubbed appearance.

Mohair

Mohair is often classed as a fashion yarn because of its distinctive hairy surface. Some people may feel it is too fluffy, and it can be an irritant, but nowadays it is often blended with other fibers to overcome this. The mohair yarns used in *Luxury Knits* are mixed with wool and silk to give a finer appearance and a refined, luxurious feel.

Cotton

Cotton is made from a natural plant fiber and, although historically used as a summer yarn, is warm in the winter and cool in the summer. It generally has a smooth appearance and can be crisp or soft depending on the manufacturing process. Cotton is good for showing stitch detail and, depending on how it is finished, can have a matte or mercerized glazed effect.

Linen

Linen is made from the stem of the flax plant, and is very strong and washes well. It absorbs moisture, so it is often good in hot climates. However, linen can be stiff and has a tendency to crease, so it is often blended with other fibers, such as cotton, to make it easier to work with and wear.

yarn care

If you have invested time and labor in making beautiful knitted garments and items, it is important that you care for them properly to keep them looking good. Caring for knitted pieces is easy, but luxury items can sometimes be ruined by incorrect washing.

WASHING AND DRYING YOUR KNITTING

• Check the ball band (see page 12) on your yarn for washing instructions. Natural fibers are generally better washed by hand than in a machine, but occasionally you can machine wash using a delicate wool cycle if the ball band recommends it.

• When hand washing, handle the knitted item carefully. There should be enough water to cover the piece completely and the soap should be thoroughly dissolved before immersing. Use soap flakes or a liquid wash created for hand knits and warm (not hot) water. Wash the knits gently. Do not rub or wring as this can felt them.

• Once clean, rinse well to remove any soap and gently squeeze out any excess water. Extra water can also be removed by rolling the piece in a towel or by using a delicate machine spin cycle.

• Dry the garment by laying it out flat on a towel to absorb the moisture. Smooth and pat it into shape, and leave it to dry away from direct heat, such as a radiator. When the knitting is dry, ease it into shape.

• Check the yarn label for specific instructions before pressing. Most fibers require only a little steam, and the iron should be applied gently. Alternatively, press with a dry iron over a damp cloth placed on the knitting so that the fabric is protected from the iron. Leave the knitting to cool and dry before storing.

buying yarn and substituting yarn

Gauge guide

Needle size

Yarn content

Yarn weight

Yardage

Shade and dye lot

Care instructions

It is best to buy the yarn that is suggested in the pattern. However, in some cases you may have to use a substitute yarn if the suggested yarn is not available to you. If this is the case then a number of factors are important.

The ply of the substitute yarn must be similar to the suggested yarn so that you can achieve the gauge stated in the pattern. Achieving the correct gauge is vitally important, otherwise the knitted item will be either too small or too large and your knitting will not fit together correctly.

Check that the properties of the substitute yarn will give you the effect that you want.

Check the yardage so that you know how much yarn to buy. Weight can vary for each yarn type, so the length of yarn needed is a more accurate guide to how many balls or skeins to purchase.

BALL BAND INFORMATION
A lot of the information you will need, including yardage and washing instructions, is given on the ball band.

recommended yarns

The following is a list of the yarns used for the projects in *Luxury Knits*. The yarn characteristics may help if you need to use a substitute yarn.

FINE YARNS

1. Jaeger Cashmina A fingering or sport weight blend (80% cashmere, 20% extra fine merino wool), approximately 137 yards (125m) per 25g ball.

2. Rowan Kidsilk Haze A lightweight blend (70% super kid mohair, 30% silk), approximately 229 yards (210m) per 25g ball.

3. RY Classic Cashsoft 4 ply 57% extra fine merino, 33% microfiber, 10% cashmere, approximately 197 yards (180m) per 50g ball.

4. Jaeger Siena 4 ply 100% mercerized cotton, approximately 153 yards (140m) per 50g ball.

5. Rowan 4 ply Soft 100% merino wool, approximately 191 yards (175m) per 50g ball.

6. Jaeger Matchmaker Merino 4 ply 100% merino wool, approximately 200 yards (183m) per 50g ball.

MEDIUM YARNS

7. Jaeger Trinity A DK weight blend (40% silk, 35% cotton, 25% polyamide), approximately 218 yards (200m) per 50g ball.

8. Rowan Summer Tweed An aran weight blend (70% silk, 30% cotton), approximately 137 yards (125m) per 50g ball.

9. Debbie Bliss Cashmerino Aran An aran weight blend (55% merino wool, 33% microfiber, 12% cashmere), approximately 99 yards (90m) per 50g ball.

CHUNKY YARNS

10. Jaeger Extra Fine Merino Chunky A chunky weight, 100% merino wool, approximately 66 yards (63m) per 50g ball.

11. Debbie Bliss Cashmerino Super Chunky A chunky weight blend (55% merino wool, 33% microfiber, 12% cashmere), approximately 82 yards (75m) per 100g ball.

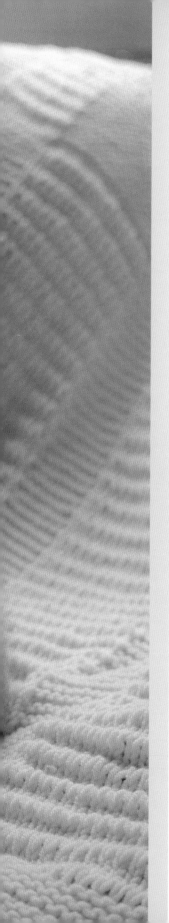

CHAPTER 1

exquisite gifts and accessories

This section includes ideas for simple, easy-to-knit pieces and small items that have a feeling of uniqueness, luxury, and comfort. Create a comfort zone with a cozy throw, pillow, and scarves. Make decorative accessories and exquisite gifts for yourself and your friends, using the finest silk mohair, refined merino wools, and cashmere blended yarns.

drawstring bags

These **soft, pretty drawstring** bags in two different sizes are ideal for storing keepsakes and special items.

large bag

MATERIALS

Jaeger Cashmina. Shade 004
  Parma. 3 x 25g balls
  (137 yds, 125m per ball).

1 pair size 3 (3.25mm) needles.

GAUGE

28 sts and 36 rows = 4 x 4"
  (10 x 10cm) over stockinette
  stitch on size 3 (3.25mm)
  needles, or needles required to
  obtain this gauge.

PATTERN

Cast on 58 sts.

Rows 1–4 Knit (garter stitch).

Rows 5–26 Work in St st starting with a k row.

Rows 27–29 Knit.

Row 30 (make eyelets for drawstring) * P2tog, yo, p1, repeat from * to last st, p1.

Rows 31–33 Knit.

Row 34 Purl.

Rows 35–106 Work in St st starting with a k row.
Change to garter stitch and work 1½" (4cm) for bottom of bag.
Change to St st and work 72 rows starting with a k row.
Make eyelets for drawstring by repeating rows 27–34.
Work rows 5–26 again.
Work rows 1–4 again.
Bind off.

FINISHING

Weave in any loose ends. Join side seams.

Make drawstring

Cut 6 lengths of yarn 32" (81cm) long. Use 2 lengths per strand and braid. Make knots at each end to hold, leaving 2" (5cm) as tassels.

SIZES	
SMALL BAG	LARGE BAG
Width	
6" (15cm)	8" (20cm)
Depth	
8" (20cm)	11" (28cm)

ABBREVIATIONS See page 126

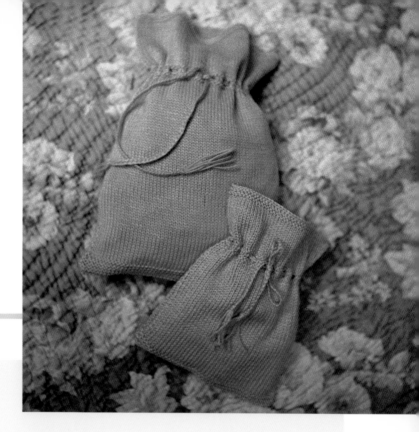

small bag

MATERIALS

RY Classic Cashsoft 4 ply.
  Shade 421 Roselake. 1 x 50g
  ball (197 yds, 180m per ball).

1 pair size 3 (3.25mm) needles.

GAUGE

28 sts and 36 rows = 4 x 4"
(10 x 10cm) over stockinette
stitch on size 3 (3.25mm)
needles, or needles required to
obtain this gauge.

PATTERN

Cast on 43 sts.

Rows 1–4 Knit (garter stitch).

Rows 5–18 Work in St st starting with a k row.

Rows 19–21 Knit.

Row 22 (make eyelets for drawstring) * P2tog, yo, p1,
repeat from * to last st, p1.

Row 23–25 Knit.

Row 26 Purl.

Rows 27–70 Work in St st starting with a k row.

Change to garter stitch and work 1¼" (3cm) for bottom of bag.

Change to St st and work 44 rows starting with a k row.

Make eyelets for drawstring by repeating rows 19–26.

Work rows 5–18 again.

Work rows 1–4 again.

Bind off.

FINISHING

Weave in any loose ends. Join side seams.

Make drawstring

Cut 6 lengths of yarn 24" (61cm) long. Use 2 lengths per
strand and braid. Make knots at each end to hold, leaving
2" (5cm) as tassels.

bed socks

Bed socks in a blend of *cashmere and mohair* provide the ultimate in comfort. An easy-knit construction means no complications with sets of needles.

MATERIALS

Debbie Bliss Cashmerino Aran.
  Shade 603.
  3 x 50g balls (99 yds, 90m per ball).

1 pair size 7 (4.5mm) and 1 pair size 9 (5.5mm) needles.

GAUGE

19 sts and 25 rows = 4 x 4" (10 x 10cm) over stockinette stitch using size 9 (5.5mm) needles, or needles required to obtain this gauge.

ABBREVIATIONS See page 126

PATTERN

LEFT SOCK

Cast on 40 sts using smaller needles.

Rows 1–4 Knit.

Rows 5–30 *K2, p2, repeat from * to end.

Rows 31–34 Knit.

Change to larger needles and work 19 rows in St st, beg with a knit row.

Shape heel

Row 1 (WS) P1, k18, p1, turn.

Row 2 K1, p17, k1, turn.

Row 3 P1, k16, p1, turn.

Row 4 K1, p15, k1, turn.

Rows 5–13 Cont decs as established (*Row 13* P1, k6, p1) – 8 sts.

Row 14 K1, p7, k1, turn.

Row 15 P1, k8, p1, turn.

Row 16 K1, p9, k1, turn.

Rows 17–24 Cont incs as established – 19 sts.

Row 25 P1, k18, purl to end.

Work 44 rows across all sts in St st, starting with a knit row – 40 sts.

Shape toe
Row 1 (RS) (K1, s1, k1, psso, p14, k2tog, k1) twice – 36 sts.
Row 2 (P2, k14, p2) twice.
Row 3 (K1, s1, k1, psso, p12, k2tog, k1) twice – 32 sts.
Row 4 (P2, k12, p2) twice.
Rows 5–10 Cont decs as established – 20 sts.
Bind off.

RIGHT SOCK
Using smaller needles cast on 40 sts and work rows 1–34 as for left sock.
Change to larger needles and work 20 rows in St st, beg with a knit row.

Shape heel
Row 1 (RS) K1, p18, k1, turn.
Row 2 P1, k17, p1, turn.
Row 3 K1, p16, k1, turn.
Row 4 P1, k15, p1, turn.
Rows 5–13 Cont decs as established (*Row 13* k1, p6, k1) – 8 sts.
Row 14 P1, k7, p1, turn.
Row 15 K1, p8, k1, turn.
Row 16 P1, k9, p1, turn.
Rows 17–24 Cont incs as established – 19 sts.
Row 25 K1, p18, knit to end.
Work 43 rows across all sts in St st, starting with a purl row.

Shape toe
Work as for left sock.

FINISHING
Weave in any loose ends. Sew toe and side seams.

hat and scarf

This *fine merino wool and mohair silk* hat and scarf set, worked in simple garter stitch, is a classic accessory combination. Stylish detailing enhances the sense of luxury.

hat

MATERIALS

Rowan Kidsilk Haze. Shade 598 Toffee. 1 x 25g ball (229 yds, 210m per ball).

Rowan 4 ply Soft. Shade 376 Nippy. 1 x 50g ball (191 yds, 175m per ball).

Use 1 strand of Rowan Kidsilk Haze and 1 strand of Rowan 4 ply Soft together throughout.

1 pair size 6 (4mm) and 1 pair size 3 (3.25mm) needles.

GAUGE

22 sts and 32 rows = 4 x 4" (10 x 10cm) over stockinette stitch and one strand each of Rowan Kidsilk Haze and Rowan 4 ply Soft on size 6 (4mm) needles, or needles required to obtain this gauge.

PATTERN

Using smaller needles, cast on 124 sts.
Work 4 rows in St st starting with a k row.
Row 5 * P2, k2, rep from * to end.
Repeat row 5 nine more times.

Change to larger needles and work in garter stitch as follows:
Row 15 Knit.
Row 16 * K4, inc, k3, inc, repeat from * to last 7 sts, inc, k6 – 151 sts on needle.
Cont straight in garter stitch until work measures 6" (15cm).

SIZE
Circumference 22" (56cm)

ABBREVIATIONS See page 126

Shape top

Row 1 K1, * k2tog, k13, repeat from * to end.
Row 2 Knit.
Row 3 K1, *k2tog, k12, repeat from * to end.
Row 4 Knit.
Row 5 K1, * k2tog, k11, repeat from * to end.
Row 6 Knit.
Cont decreases as established until 11 sts remain.
Next row K1, * k2tog, repeat from * to end.
Thread yarn through rem sts, pull tightly and
fasten securely.

FINISHING

Weave in any loose ends. Join side seam.

scarf

MATERIALS

Rowan Kidsilk Haze. Shade 598 Toffee.
  2 x 25g balls (229 yds, 210m per ball).

Rowan 4 ply Soft. Shade 376 Nippy.
  3 x 50g balls (191 yds, 175m per ball).

Use 1 strand of Rowan Kidsilk Haze and 1 strand
  of Rowan 4 ply Soft together throughout.

1 pair size 8 (5mm) needles.

GAUGE

17 sts and 32 rows = 4 x 4" (10 x 10cm) over
  garter stitch and one strand each of Rowan
  Kidsilk Haze and Rowan 4 ply Soft together on
  size 8 (5mm) needles, or needles required to
  obtain this gauge.

PATTERN

Cast on 41 sts.
Work in garter stitch (every row knit) until scarf
measures 55" (140cm).
Bind off.

FINISHING

Weave in any loose ends. Press lightly using a warm
iron over a damp cloth.

SIZE	
Width 9" (23cm)	
Length 55" (140cm)	

scarf and mittens

Delicate pastel hues and a wonderfully *soft merino and cashmere* yarn blend are perfect for this lacy scarf and matching lace-panelled mittens.

scarf

MATERIALS
Debbie Bliss Cashmerino Aran.
  Shade 202. 4 x 50g balls
  (99 yds, 90m per ball).

1 pair size 8 (5mm) needles.

Optional: 4.4 yds (4m)
  satin ribbon.

GAUGE
18 sts and 24 rows = 4 x 4"
(10 x 10cm) over stockinette
stitch on size 8 (5mm) needles,
or needles required to obtain
this gauge.

PATTERN
Cast on 32 sts.
Knit 2 rows.
Change to lace patt as follows.
Row 1 K3, *yo, s1, k1, psso, k4, k2tog, yo, k1,
repeat from * to last 2 sts, k2.
Row 2 K2, p2, *k6, p3, repeat from * to last 10 sts,
k6, p2, k2.
Row 3 K4, *yo, s1, k1, psso, k2, k2tog, yo, k3,
repeat from * to last 10 sts, yo, s1, k1, psso, k2,
k2tog, yo, k4.
Row 4 K2, p3, *k4, p5, repeat from * to last 9 sts,
k4, p3, k2.
Row 5 K5, *yo, s1, k1, psso, k2tog, yo, k5, repeat
from * to last 9 sts, yo, s1, k1, psso, k2tog, yo, k5.
Row 6 K2, p4, *k2, p7, repeat from * to last 8 sts,
k2, p4, k2.
Rows 1–6 form patt repeat.
Cont in patt until work measures approx 58½"
(149cm), ending with a row 6.
Knit 2 rows.
Bind off.

FINISHING
Weave in any loose ends. Press lightly using
a warm iron over a damp cloth.

SIZE
Width 7½" (19cm)
Length 59" (150cm)

ABBREVIATIONS See page 126

mittens

MATERIALS
Debbie Bliss Cashmerino Aran. Shade 202.
1 x 50g ball (100 yds, 90m per ball).

1 pair size 8 (5mm) needles.

GAUGE
18 sts and 24 rows = 4 x 4" (10 x 10cm) over
stockinette stitch on size 8 (5mm) needles, or
needles required to obtain this gauge.

PATTERN
LEFT MITTEN
Cast on 35 sts.
Knit 3 rows.
Change to patt as follows.
Row 1 (RS) K22, yo, s1, k1, psso, k4, k2tog,
yo, k5.
Row 2 P6, k6, p23.
Row 3 K23, yo, s1, k1, psso, k2, k2tog, yo, k6.
Row 4 P7, k4, p24.
Row 5 K24, yo, s1, k1, psso, k2tog, yo, k7.
Row 6 P8, k2, p25.
Rows 1–6 form patt repeat.
Rows 7–20 Work in patt.

Shape thumb gusset
Row 21 (RS) K15, inc, k1, inc, patt to end – 37 sts.
Row 22 Patt.
Row 23 K15, inc, k3, inc, patt to end – 39 sts.
Row 24 Patt.
Row 25 K15, inc, k5, inc, patt to end – 41 sts.
Row 26 Patt.
Row 27 K15, inc, k7, inc, patt to end – 43 sts.
Row 28 Patt.

Work thumb
Row 29 (RS) K26, turn, cast on 1 st – 27 sts.
Row 30 P12, turn, cast on 1 st – 13 sts.
Row 31 K13.
**On these 13 sts work 11 rows in St st.

Shape top of thumb
Row 1 (RS) (K1, k2tog) four times, k1 – 9 sts.
Row 2 Purl.
Row 3 (K2tog) four times, k1 – 5 sts.
Thread yarn through rem sts, pull together tightly
and fasten.
Join thumb seam.

Rejoin yarn to mitten at thumb base.
With RS facing, pick up 2 sts from thumb base, patt
across rem sts of row 29 – 34 sts.
Rows 30–54 Work in patt.

Shape top
Row 55 (RS) (K1, s1, k1, psso, k11, k2tog, k1)
twice – 30 sts.
Row 56 Purl.
Row 57 (K1, s1, k1, psso, k9, k2tog, k1) twice –
26 sts.
Row 58 Purl.
Row 59 (K1, s1, k1, psso, k7, k2tog, k1) twice – 22 sts.
Row 60 Purl.
Row 61 (K1, sl, k1, psso, k5, k2tog, k1) twice –
18 sts.
Bind off.

SIZE
To fit an average hand.

RIGHT MITTEN

Cast on 35 sts.

Knit 3 rows.

Change to patt as follows.

Row 1 (RS) K5, yo, s1, k1, psso, k4, k2tog, yo, k22.

Row 2 P23, k6, p6.

Row 3 K6, yo, s1, k1, psso, k2, k2tog, yo, k23.

Row 4 P24, k4, p7.

Row 5 K7, yo, s1, k1, psso, k2tog, yo, k24.

Row 6 P25, k2, p8.

Rows 1–6 form patt repeat.

Rows 7–20 Work in patt.

Shape thumb gusset

Row 21 (RS) Patt 17, inc, k1, inc, knit to end –
37 sts.

Row 22 Patt.

Row 23 Patt 17, inc, k3, inc, knit to end – 39 sts.

Row 24 Patt.

Row 25 Patt 17, inc, k5, inc, knit to end – 41 sts.

Row 26 Patt.

Row 27 Patt 17, inc, k7, inc, knit to end – 43 sts.

Row 28 Patt.

Work thumb

Row 29 (RS) Patt 28, turn, cast on 1 st – 29 sts.

Row 30 P12, turn, cast on 1 st – 30 sts.

Row 31 K13.

Work from ** to end as for left mitten.

FINISHING

Join top and side seams. Weave in any loose ends.
Optional: Thread each end of the satin ribbon
through the lace paneling at the top of each mitten
and tie in bows (*see photograph*).

blanket and pillow

Create a comfort zone with a *super-chunky and super-soft merino wool* blanket, worked in a striking garter and drop stitch pattern, and a cozy merino wool and kid silk pillow in a beautiful blend of colors.

blanket

MATERIALS
Jaeger Extra Fine Merino Chunky. Shade 21 Pearl. 18 x 50g balls (69 yds, 63m per ball).

1 pair size 10½ (6.5mm) needles.

GAUGE
13 sts and 15 rows = 4 x 4" (10 x 10cm) over stockinette stitch on size 10½ (6.5mm) needles, or needles required to obtain this gauge.

SIZE
Width 63" (158cm)
Length 59" (150cm)

PATTERN
Cast on 168 sts.
Rows 1–4 Knit.
Row 5 K4, (k16 wy2rn, k8) six times, k16 wy2rn, k4.
Row 6 K4, (p16 dropping extra loop, k8) six times, p16 dropping extra loop, k4.
Row 7 Knit.
Row 8 K4, (p16, k8) six times, p16, k4.
Rows 9–28 Repeat rows 5–8 five times.
Row 29 K20, (k8 wy2rn, k16) six times, k4.
Row 30 K20, (p8 dropping extra loop, k16) six times, k4.
Row 31 Knit.
Row 32 K20, (p8, k16) six times, k4.
Rows 33–52 Repeat rows 29–32 five times.
Rows 53–56 Repeat rows 5–8.
Repeat rows 5–8 until this section measures approx 31" (78cm), ending with a row 8.
Work rows 29–52 again.
Work rows 5–28 again.
Knit 4 rows.
Bind off.

FINISHING
Weave in any loose ends. Press lightly using a warm iron over a damp cloth.

ABBREVIATIONS See page 126
SPECIAL ABBREVIATION wy2rn = winding yarn twice round needle. See page 30.

pillow

MATERIALS

Rowan Kidsilk Haze. Shade 600 Dewberry and
   Shade 605 Smoke. 2 x 25g balls (229 yds,
   210m) per ball in each shade.

Rowan 4 ply Soft. Shade 376 Nippy.
   3 x 50g balls (191 yds, 175m) per ball.

Use 1 strand of each of the Rowan Kidsilk Haze
   yarns and 1 strand of Rowan 4 ply Soft together
   throughout.

1 pair size 10 (6mm) needles.

Pillow form 18" (45.75cm) square.

GAUGE

16 sts and 21 rows = 4 x 4" (10 x 10cm) over
   stockinette stitch and one strand each of Rowan
   Kidsilk Haze and Rowan 4 ply Soft together on
   size 10 (6mm) needles, or needles required to
   obtain this gauge.

PATTERN

FRONT

Cast on 73 sts.
Knit 10 rows.
Row 11 Knit.
Row 12 K7, p59, k7.
Repeat rows 11 and 12 until work measures
16½" (42cm), ending with a row 12.
Knit 10 rows.
Bind off.

BACK

Cast on 73 sts.
Work 18" (45.75cm) in stockinette stitch.
Bind off.

FINISHING

Place back and front RS together and sew around
3 edges. Turn RS out. Insert pillow form. Carefully
join 4th edge.

SIZE
18" (45.75cm) **square**

WY2RN This is a very easy drop stitch and is created by wrapping the yarn around the needle more times than usual.

Insert the right-hand needle into the next stitch from front to
back. Instead of holding the yarn at the back of the work,
which is usual when working a knit stitch, bring the yarn
forward over the needle twice, then complete the stitch in the
usual way.

When working purl stitches on the next row (wrong side of
work), work only into the first stitch. When you have purled
the stitch and are ready to drop it off the left needle, let the
loop wrapped around the needle drop off as well. The drop
stitch is then completed.

baby sweater

This beautiful baby's sweater, a simple, modern piece for either a baby girl or boy, is knitted in the *softest 4 ply cashmere and merino* wool.

MATERIALS
RY Classic Cashsoft 4 ply. Shade 433 Cream. 3 (3) x 50g balls (197 yds, 180m per ball).

1 pair size 3 (3.25mm) needles.

GAUGE
28 sts and 36 rows = 4 x 4" (10 x 10cm) over stockinette stitch on size 3 (3.25mm) needles, or needles required to obtain this gauge.

SIZES

	3–6 MONTHS	6–12 MONTHS
To fit chest	18" (45.75cm)	20" (51cm)
Actual size	20½" (52cm)	22¾" (58cm)
Back length	9½" (24cm)	11" (28cm)
Sleeve seam	6¼" (16cm)	7¼" (18.5cm)

GARMENT SIZING See page 124
ABBREVIATIONS See page 126

PATTERN
BACK
Cast on 76 (82) sts.
Work in garter stitch until back measures 6 (7)" [15 (18)cm].

Shape armhole
Bind off 3 sts at beg of next 2 rows.
Dec 1 st at both ends of every other row until 66 (70) sts remain.
Cont in garter stitch until work measures 9½ (11)" [24 (28)cm].

Shape neck and shoulders
RIGHT SIDE OF NECK
Row 1 Bind off 5 sts, k16 (17), turn.
Row 2 Bind off 3 sts, knit to end.
Row 3 Bind off 5 sts, knit to end.
Row 4 Bind off 2 sts, knit to end.
Bind off rem 6 (7) sts.

LEFT SIDE
Rejoin yarn to rem sts at neck.
Bind off 24 (26) sts, knit to end. Work to match first side, reversing all shaping.

FRONT

Cast on 76 (82) sts.

Row 1 (RS) Knit.

Row 2 K23 (26), * p6, k6, repeat from * once, p6, k23 (26).

These 2 rows form the patt repeat.

Cont in patt until work measures 5½ (6½)" [14 (16.5)cm], ending with a row 1.

Divide for neck opening

RIGHT SIDE OF NECK

WS facing. Patt 41 (44), turn and work on these sts.

Cont in patt until work measures 6 (7)" [15 (18)cm], ending with a row 1.

Shape armhole

WS facing. Bind off 3 sts beg of next row.

Dec 1 st at armhole edge on next and then every other row until 36 (38) sts remain.

Cont in patt until work measures 8 (9½)" [20 (24)cm], ending with a row 2.

Shape neck

RS facing. Bind off 12 (13) sts, patt to end.

Dec at neck edge on every row until 16 (17) sts remain.

Cont without shaping until work measures the same as back at shoulder, ending with a RS row.

Shape shoulder

WS facing. Bind off 5 sts at beg of next and foll WS row.

Work 1 row.

Bind off.

LEFT SIDE OF NECK

Rejoin yarn to rem sts at neck edge. Cast on 6 sts for underlap of neck, work as follows.

Row 1 (WS) K12, p6, k23 (26).

Row 2 Knit.

These 2 rows form patt for left side of neck.

Cont in patt and work to match first side, reversing all shaping.

SLEEVES

Cast on 40 (42) sts.

Row 1 Knit.

Row 2 K5 (6), * p6, k6, repeat from * once, p6, k5 (6).

These 2 rows form patt repeat.

Cont in patt, inc each end of 11th and every foll 10th row to 48 (50) sts, working extra sts in garter stitch.

Cont working straight until sleeve measures 6¼ (7¼)" [16 (18.5)cm].

Shape armholes

Bind off 2 (3) sts beg next 2 rows.

Dec each end of next and every other row until 30 sts remain.

Bind off.

NECKBAND

Join shoulder seams.

With RS facing, pick up and knit 24 (26) sts from right front neck, 34 (36) sts from back neck, 24 (26) sts from left front neck – 82 (88) sts.

Work ½" (1cm) in garter stitch.

Bind off.

FINISHING

Weave in any loose ends. Join side seams, leaving 1½" (4cm) open at hem. Join sleeve seams. Line up sleeve with armhole and stitch. Press lightly using a warm iron over a damp cloth.

Optional: Embroidery (*see photograph*). Using one strand of yarn, work a vertical row of 9 cross stitches up the central front panel. Each stitch should be approximately 4 stitches across and 7 rows high. Complete each cross stitch with a stitch over its center.

blanket and booties

Precious baby booties and a matching super-soft blanket, made from *garter stitch and stockinette squares*, create a gorgeous gift for a newborn or a comforting treat for an older baby.

blanket

MATERIALS
Jaeger Cashmina. Shade 042 Verdigris. 9 x 25g balls (137 yds, 125m) per ball.

1 pair size 3 (3.25mm) needles.

GAUGE
28 sts and 36 rows = 4 x 4" (10 x 10cm) over stockinette stitch on size 3 (3.25mm) needles, or needles required to obtain this gauge.

PATTERN
Cast on 196 sts.
Row 1 Knit.
Row 2 (K28, p28) three times, k28.
Rows 3–36 Repeat rows 1 and 2 seventeen times.
Row 37 Knit.
Row 38 (P28, k28) three times, p28.
Rows 39–72 Repeat rows 37 and 38 seventeen times.
These 72 rows form the pattern.
Work rows 1–72 twice more.
Work rows 1–36 once more.
Bind off.

FINISHING
Weave in any loose ends.

SIZE
27½ x 27½" (70 x 70cm)

ABBREVIATIONS See page 126

booties

MATERIALS

Jaeger Cashmina. Shade 030 Ecru (main color = MC). 2 x 25g balls (137 yds, 125m) per ball.

(Optional) Jaeger Cashmina. Shade 042 Verdigris (contrasting color = CC). 1 x 25g ball (137 yds, 125m) per ball.

1 pair size 3 (3.25mm) needles.

2 knitting markers.

Safety pin.

GAUGE

28 sts and 36 rows = 4 x 4" (10 x 10cm) over stockinette stitch on size 3 (3.25mm) needles, or needles required to obtain this gauge.

PATTERN

Start at heel of sole

Cast on 5 sts using MC and work in garter stitch.

Row 1 Knit.

Row 2 Inc, knit to last st, inc.

Rows 3 and 4 Repeat rows 1 and 2.

Rows 5–16 Work in garter stitch inc 1 st at each end of 8th and 12th rows.

LARGE SIZE ONLY Inc 1 st at each end of row 16 – 13 (15) sts.

Cont in garter stitch until work measures 2½ (3¼)" [6.5 (8)cm]. Place marker 1 at each end of last row.

Shape toe

Rows 1 and 2 Knit, dec 1 st at each end of row.

Rows 3 and 4 Bind off 2 sts, knit to end – 5 (7) sts.

Row 5 Knit.

Shape upper part of toe

Row 1 K0 (1) inc in next 5 sts, k0 (1) – 10 (12) sts.

Row 2 (K1, inc) 5 (6) times – 15 (18) sts.

Row 3 Knit.

Row 4 (K2, inc) 4 (5) times, k3 – 19 (23) sts.

Row 5 Knit.

Row 6 K0 (2), (k3, inc) 4 times, k3 (5) – 23 (27) sts. Place marker 2 at each end of row.

Work a further 1½ (1¾)" [4 (4.5)cm] in garter stitch.

Divide for ankle

Next row K9 (11), turn and cont on these sts until work measures 3¼ (4)" [8 (10)cm] from marker 2. Bind off.

Place center 5 sts on a safety pin.

Rejoin yarn to rem sts at center and work to match first side.

Top of bootie

With RS facing and using MC, pick up and knit 16 (19) sts from heel to ankle divide, 5 sts from safety pin and 16 (19) sts from ankle divide to heel – 37 (43) sts.

Next row (WS) Knit.

Work 2 (4) rows in stockinette stitch, starting with a knit row.

Next row Change to CC and work 2 rows in stockinette stitch.

Change to MC and work 2 rows in stockinette stitch.

Change to CC and knit 4 rows.

Bind off.

FINISHING

Weave in any loose ends. Join leg seam. Line up upper around sole, matching markers. Sew sole to upper.

SIZE	
SMALL	LARGE
Foot length	
3¼" (8cm)	4" (10cm)

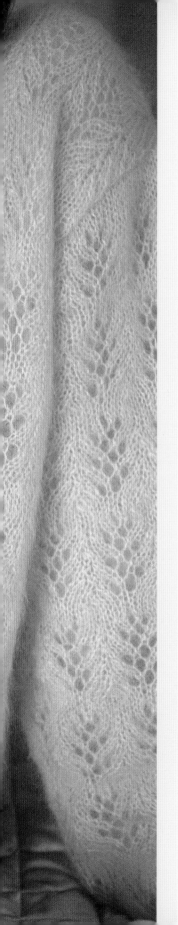

CHAPTER 2

winter indulgence

This collection of timeless designs includes
beautifully detailed sweaters, softly tailored
jackets, and draped and wrapped cardigans.
These comfortable, classic shapes conjure ease and
relaxation, combined with sumptuous yarn blends
of cashmere, silk, and merino wool that are ideal
for winter luxury whether indoors or outside.

v-neck sweater

This comfortable V-neck sweater in **_merino wool and cashmere_** is a classic garment, enhanced by fully fashioned detailing around the neck and in the raglan shaping.

MATERIALS

RY Classic Cashsoft 4 ply. Shade 423 Monet. 8 (8, 9, 9, 10) x 50g balls (197 yds, 180m per ball).

1 pair size 3 (3.25mm) needles.

Stitch holders.

GAUGE

28 sts and 36 rows = 4 x 4" (10 x 10cm) over stockinette stitch on size 3 (3.25mm) needles, or needles required to obtain this gauge.

PATTERN
BACK

Cast on 140 (152, 161, 170, 182) sts.

Row 1 (RS) * P2, k1, repeat from * to last 2 sts, p2.

Row 2 * K2, p1, repeat from * to last 2 sts, k2.

These 2 rows form the rib patt.

Cont in patt until work measures 2½" (6.5cm), ending with a row 2.

SIZE				
SMALL	MEDIUM	LARGE	XL	XXL
To fit bust				
34–36"	36–38"	38–40"	41–44"	46"
(86–91.5cm)	(91.5–96.5cm)	(96.5–102cm)	(104–112cm)	(117cm)
Actual size				
38" (96.5cm)	41" (104cm)	44" (112cm)	47" (119.5cm)	50" (127cm)
Back length				
22½" (57cm)	22¾" (58cm)	23¼" (59cm)	24½" (61cm)	25" (63.5cm)
Sleeve seam				
19" (48cm)	19" (48cm)	19" (48cm)	19" (48cm)	19" (48cm)

GARMENT SIZING See page 124
ABBREVIATIONS See page 126

Inc 1 st each end on SMALL and EXTRA LARGE sizes and inc 1 st at end on LARGE size on last row – 142 (152, 162, 172, 182) sts.

Change to St st, beg with a knit row.

Dec 1 st at each end of 13th row and every foll 14th row to 136 (146, 156, 166, 176) sts.

Cont without shaping until work measures 14¼" (36cm).

Shape armholes

Rows 1 and 2 Bind off 5 (7, 9, 11, 13) sts at beg of row.**

Row 3 K2, p2, wyib, s1, k3, psso, knit to last 4 sts, p2, k2.

Row 4 P2, k2, wyif, s1, p3, psso, purl to last 4 sts, k2, p2.

Repeat rows 3 and 4 until 44 (46, 48, 50, 52) sts remain.

Leave sts on a holder.

FRONT

Work as for back to **.

Repeat rows 3 and 4 of armhole shaping until 117 (123, 129, 135, 141) sts remain, ending with a row 3.

Divide for neck

Next row P2, k2, wyif, s1, p3, psso, p51 (54, 57, 60, 63), k3, wyif, s1, p3, psso, p47 (50, 53, 56, 59), k2, p2.

LEFT SIDE OF NECK

Working on first 58 (61, 64, 67, 70) sts, cont as follows:

Row 1 K2, p2, wyib, s1, k3, psso, knit to last 3 sts, p3.

Row 2 K3, purl to last 4 sts, k2, p2.

Row 3 Repeat row 1.

Row 4 K3, wyif, s1, p3, psso, purl to last 4 sts, k2, p2.

Repeat rows 1–4 until 12 sts remain, ending with a row 4.

Cont as follows:

Row 1 K2, p2, wyib, s1, k3, psso, k1, p3.

Row 2 K3, p4, k2, p2.

Row 3 K2, p2, wyib, s1, k1, k2tog, psso, p3.

Row 4 K3, p2, k2, p2.

Row 5 K2, p2, wyib, s1, k2tog, psso, p2.

Row 6 K2, p1, k2, p2.

Row 7 K2, p2, p2tog, p1.

Row 8 K4, p2.

Row 9 K2, p2tog twice.

Row 10 Bind off.

RIGHT SIDE OF NECK

With RS facing, rejoin yarn to rem sts at neck edge, p3, wyib, s1, k3, psso, knit to last 4 sts, p2, k2. Work to match left side of neck, reversing all shaping.

SLEEVES

Cast on 74 (74, 80, 80, 86) sts and work 1½" (4cm) in rib as on back.

Change to St st, beg with a knit row.
Inc 1 st at each end of 9th and every foll 12th (12th, 10th, 8th, 8th) row to 90 (98, 106, 114, 122) sts.
Cont without shaping until work measures 19" (48cm).

Shape sleeve cap

Rows 1–2 Bind off 5 (7, 9, 11, 13) sts, work to end.

Row 3 K2, p2, wyib, s1, k3, psso, knit to last 4 sts, p2, k2.

Row 4 P2, k2, wyif, s1, p3, psso, purl to last 4 sts, k2, p2.

Row 5 K2, p2, knit to last 4 sts, p2, k2.

Row 6 P2, k2, purl to last 4 sts, k2, p2.

Repeat rows 3–6 until 66 (70, 74, 78, 82) sts remain.

Repeat rows 3 and 4 until 14 sts remain.

ALL SIZES

Left sleeve Cut yarn and leave sts on holder.

Right sleeve DO NOT cut yarn and leave sts on needle.

NECKBAND

With RS facing, purl across 14 sts of right sleeve, 44 (46, 48, 50, 52) sts of back and 14 sts of left sleeve.
Work 2 rows St st, beg with a knit row.
Bind off.

FINISHING

Weave in any loose ends. Join raglan seams. Join side and sleeve seams. Press lightly using a warm iron over a damp cloth.

wraparound cardigan

Worked in a ***super-soft, chunky merino and cashmere*** yarn, this wraparound cardigan, with shawl collar, tie belt, and diagonal stitch detailing, is the ultimate in style and comfort.

MATERIALS
Debbie Bliss Cashmerino Super Chunky. Shade 15. 12 (12, 13, 13, 14) x 100g balls (82 yds, 75m per ball).

1 pair size 10½ (6.5mm) and 1 pair size 11 (8mm) needles.

GAUGE
12 sts and 17 rows = 4 x 4" (10 x 10cm) over stockinette stitch using size 11 (8mm) needles, or needles required to obtain this gauge.

PATTERN
BACK
Cast on 59 (63, 67, 73, 79) sts using smaller needles and, working in hem patt, follow rows 1 to 10 from Back chart.
Change to larger needles and, working in stitch patt, follow rows 11 to 114 (114, 116, 116, 118) from Back chart.

RIGHT AND LEFT FRONTS
Cast on 35 (37, 39, 42, 45) sts using size smaller needles and, working in hem patt, follow rows 1 to 10 from appropriate chart.
Change to larger needles and, working in stitch patt, follow rows 11 to 112/113 (112/113, 114/115, 114/115, 116/117) from appropriate Front chart.

SIZES				
SMALL	MEDIUM	LARGE	XL	XXL
To fit bust				
34" (86cm)	35–37" (89–94cm)	38–40" (96.5–102cm)	41–44" (104–112cm)	45–48" (114–122cm)
Actual size				
38" (96.5cm)	41" (104cm)	44" (112cm)	47" (119.5cm)	50" (127cm)
Back length				
27" (68cm)	27" (68cm)	27½" (70cm)	28" (71cm)	28" (71cm)
Sleeve seam				
19" (48cm)	19" (48cm)	19" (48cm)	19" (48cm)	19" (48cm)

GARMENT SIZING See page 124
ABBREVIATIONS See page 126

SLEEVES

Cast on 33 (33, 35, 35, 37) sts using smaller
needles and, working in hem patt, follow rows 1–10
from Sleeve chart.

Change to larger needles and, working in stitch patt,
follow rows 11–38 from Sleeve chart – 39 (39, 41,
41, 43) sts.

Continue as follows.

Working in St st, inc 1 st at each end of 5th row and
every foll 10th row to 45 (45, 47, 47, 49) sts.

Cont without shaping until work measures 19"
(48cm).

Shape sleeve cap

Bind off 2 sts beg next 2 rows – 41 (41, 43, 43,
45) sts.

Dec 1 st at each end of next and every other row
to 31 sts.

Work 1 row.

Bind off 3 sts beg next 2 rows – 25 sts.

Bind off rem sts.

BELT

Cast on 9 sts using smaller needles.

Row 1 (K1, p1) four times, k1.

Row 2 (P1, k1) four times, p1.

Row 3 K1, p1, k2, p1, k2, p1, k1.

Row 4 P1, k1, p2, k1, p2, k1, p1.

Rows 1–4 form patt repeat.

Cont in patt until belt measures 48" (122cm).
Bind off.

FRONT BANDS AND COLLAR

RIGHT BAND

Cast on 8 sts using smaller needles and work
as folls.

Row 1 (RS) (K1, p1) three times, k2.

Row 2 P2, (k1, p1) three times.

Row 3 K1, p1, k2, p1, k3.

Row 4 P3, k1, p2, k1, p1.

Rows 1–4 form patt repeat.

Cont in patt until right band measures same as
right front to start of neck shaping, ending with
a row 1 or 3.

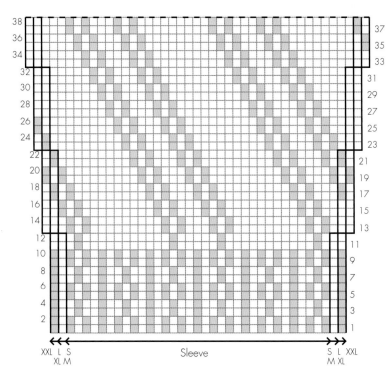

Key

☐ Knit on RS, purl on WS

▨ Purl on RS, knit on WS

Sleeve

XXL L S   S L XXL
XL M   M XL

Shape collar

With WS facing, inc beg of next row and every foll 4th row to 18 sts, working extra sts into patt as on rows 1–10 on charts.

Cont without shaping until collar fits up front shaping and halfway around back of neck.

Bind off.

LEFT BAND

Cast on 8 sts using smaller needles and work as folls.

Row 1 (RS) K2, (p1, k1) three times.

Row 2 (P1, k1) three times, p2.

Row 3 K3, p1, k2, p1, k1.

Row 4 P1, k1, p2, k1, p3.

Rows 1–4 form patt repeat.

Cont in patt and work to match right band and collar, reversing all shaping.

FINISHING

Weave in any loose ends. Join shoulder seams. Join collar at bind off. Carefully pin collar and bands to fronts and back neck. Using mattress stitch, join bands and collar to garment. Join side and sleeve seams. Ease sleeve cap into armhole and stitch into place. Make loops at side seam for belt if desired. Press lightly using a cool iron.

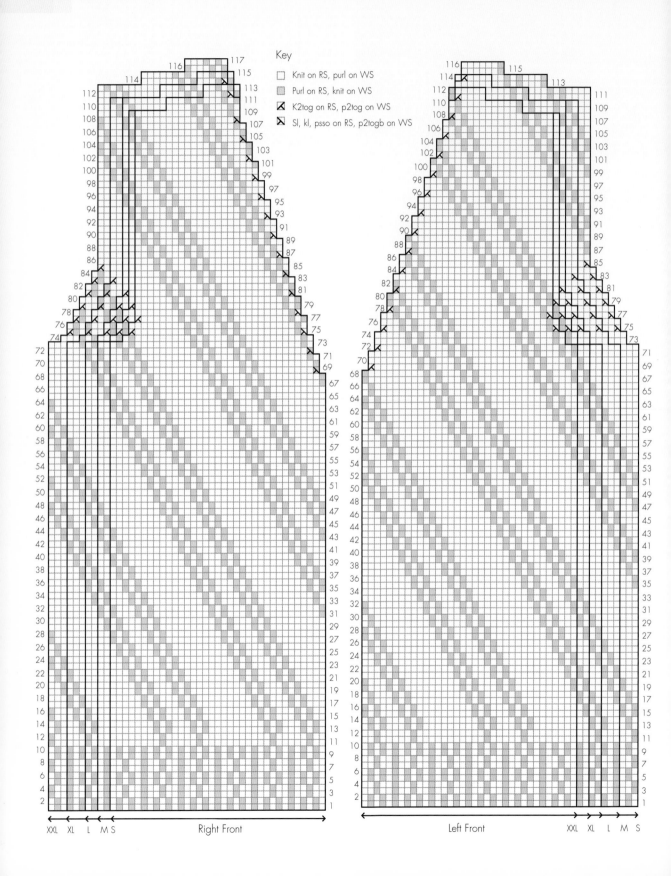

Key

☐ Knit on RS, purl on WS

▨ Purl on RS, knit on WS

◪ K2tog on RS, p2tog on WS

◪ Sl, kl, psso on RS, p2togb on WS

Right Front

XXL XL L M S

Left Front

XXL XL L M S

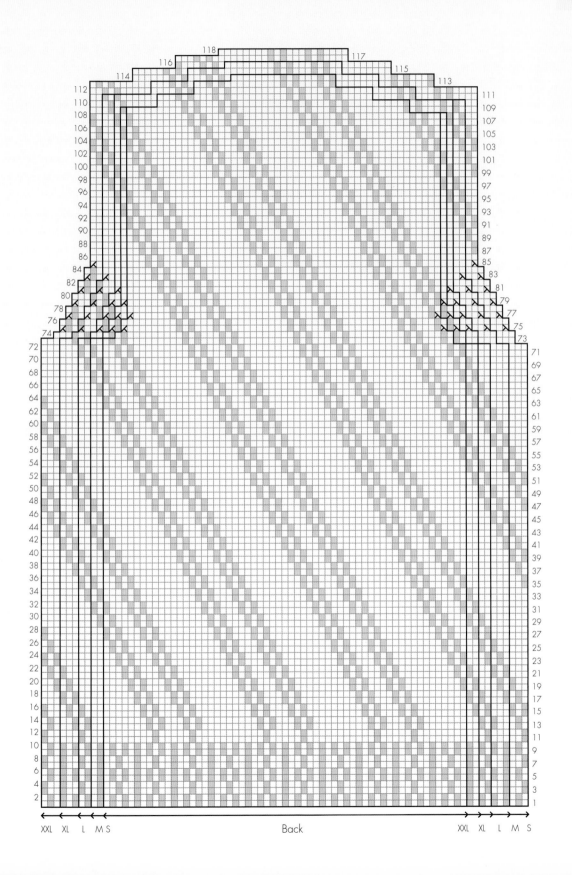

traveling stitch and rib cardigan

A *soft merino wool and cashmere* blended yarn provides a luxurious feel for this elegant cardigan, worked in traveling stitch and rib.

MATERIALS
Debbie Bliss Cashmerino Super Chunky.
  Shade 01. 11 (11, 12, 12, 13) x 100g
  balls (82 yds, 75m per ball).

1 pair size 10½ (6.5mm) and 1 pair size 11
(8mm) needles.

Stitch holder.

8 buttons.

GAUGE
12 sts and 17 rows = 4 x 4" (10 x
  10cm) over stockinette stitch using
  size 11 (8mm) needles, or needles
  required to obtain this gauge.

PATTERN
BACK
Cast on 59 (63, 69, 73, 77) sts
using smaller needles and, working
in hem patt, follow rows 1–14 from
Back chart.
Change to larger needles and, working
in stitch patt, follow rows 15–108 (108,
110, 110, 112) from Back chart.

SIZES				
SMALL	MEDIUM	LARGE	XL	XXL
To fit bust				
32–34" (81–86cm)	35–37" (89–94cm)	38–40" (96.5–102cm)	41–43" (104–109cm)	44–46" (112–117cm)
Actual size				
38" (96.5cm)	41" (104cm)	44" (112cm)	47" (119.5cm)	50" (127cm)
Back length				
25½" (65cm)	25½" (65cm)	26" (66cm)	26" (66cm)	26½" (67cm)
Sleeve seam				
19" (48cm)	19" (48cm)	19" (48cm)	19" (48cm)	19" (48cm)

GARMENT SIZING See page 124
ABBREVIATIONS See page 126

POCKET LINING

Cast on 14 sts using smaller needles and work 29 rows in St st. Leave sts on a holder.

LEFT FRONT

Cast on 27 (29, 32, 34, 36) sts using smaller needles and, working in hem patt, follow rows 1–14 from appropriate Front chart.
Change to larger needles and, working in stitch patt, follow rows 15–28 from appropriate Front chart.

Shape pocket opening

Row 29 K3 (5, 8, 10, 12), p2tog, patt 22.
Row 30 Patt 21, k2tog, turn.
Row 31 P2tog, patt 20.
Row 32 P19, k2tog, turn.
Rows 33–42 Continue decreasing as established – 10 sts.
Break yarn.

Place pocket

Row 30 Rejoin yarn to pocket sts. Purl across 14 sts of pocket lining, purl across 3 (5, 8, 10, 12) sts of front.
Rows 31–42 Work in St st.
Row 43 K18 (20, 23, 25, 27), patt 9.
Rows 44–108 (108, 110, 110, 112) Working in stitch pattern, follow chart.

RIGHT FRONT

Work to match left front, noting:
Row 29 Patt 22, p2tog, turn.
Row 30 S1, k1, psso, patt to end.

SLEEVES

Cast on 31 (31, 33, 33, 35) sts using smaller needles and, working in hem patt, follow rows 1–14 from Sleeve chart.
Change to larger needles and, working in stitch patt, follow rows 15–46 from Sleeve chart.
Cont working in St st, inc 1 st at each end of 5th row and every foll 8th row to 43 (43, 47, 47, 49) sts.

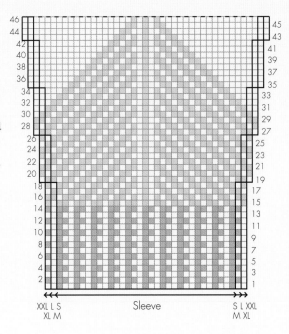

Key
□ Knit RS, purl on WS
▨ Purl on RS, knit on WS
▨ Purl on RS, knit on WS

Cont in St st without shaping until work measures 19" (48cm).

Shape sleeve cap

Bind off 2 sts at beg next 2 rows – 39 (39, 43, 43, 45) sts.
Dec 1 st at each end of next and every other row to 31 sts.
Work 1 row.
Bind off 3 sts at beg of next 2 rows – 25 sts.
Bind off.

FRONT BANDS

LEFT BAND

Cast on 9 sts using smaller needles.
Row 1 (P1, k2) three times.
Row 2 K1, (p1, k2) twice, p1, k1.

Rows 1 and 2 form patt repeat.
Cont in patt until band measures same as left front from hem to start of neck shaping, ending with a row 2. Break yarn and leave sts on holder. Mattress stitch band to left front. Mark position for 6 buttons, the first on row 5, the sixth 12 rows down from neck and the remaining four evenly spaced between.

RIGHT BAND

Cast on 9 sts using smaller needles.
Row 1 (K2, p1) three times.
Row 2 K1, (p1, k2) twice, p1, k1.
Rows 3–4 Repeat rows 1 and 2.
Row 5 Patt 3, bind off 3 sts, patt 3.
Row 6 Patt 3, cast on 3 sts, patt 3.
Cont in patt making buttonholes to match marked positions, until band measures same as right front to neck. Do not break yarn. Mattress stitch band to right front.

COLLAR

Join shoulder seams.
With RS facing and using smaller needles, patt across right band, pick up and knit 13 (13, 15, 15, 17) sts from right front neck, 21 (21, 23, 23, 25) sts from back neck and 13 (13, 15, 15, 17) sts from left front neck, patt across left band – 65 (65, 71, 71, 77) sts.
Row 1 K1, (p1, k2), to last st, p1.
Cont in patt as on front bands until collar measures 5" (12cm), making further buttonholes on rows 4 and 5 and at 4" (10cm).
Bind off in pattern.

FINISHING

Weave in any loose ends. Join side and sleeve seams. Ease sleeve cap into armhole and stitch into place. Slipstitch pocket linings into position. Sew on buttons. Press lightly using a cool iron.

Key

- ☐ Knit on RS, purl on WS
- ▨ Purl on RS, knit on WS
- ▨ Purl on RS, knit on WS
- ◣ P2tog on RS, k2tog on WS
- ◿ P2tog on RS, sl, k1, psso on WS
- ◪ K2tog on RS, p2tog on WS
- ◪ Sl, k1, psso on RS, P2togb on WS

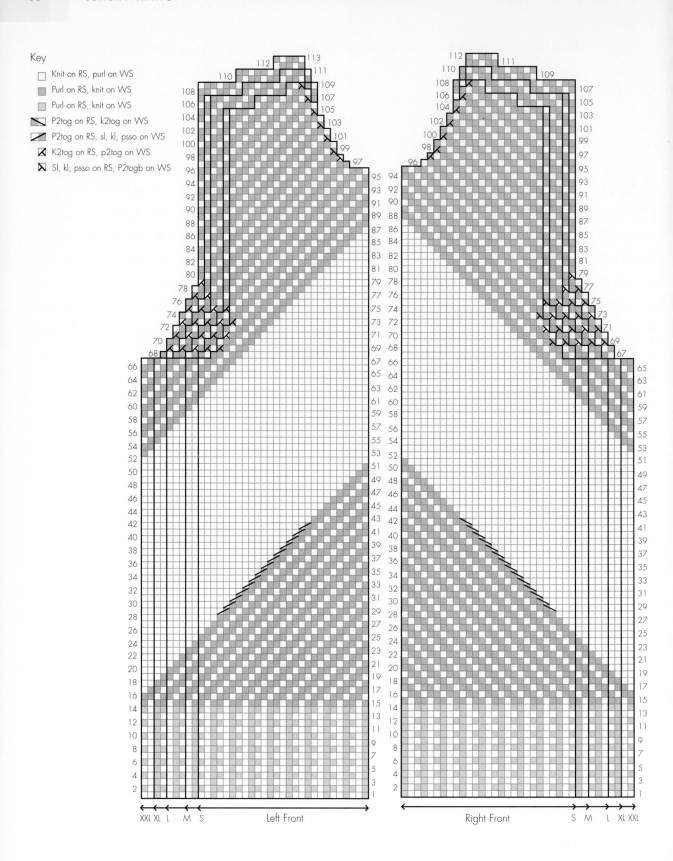

Left Front   Right Front

XXL XL L M S   S M L XL XXL

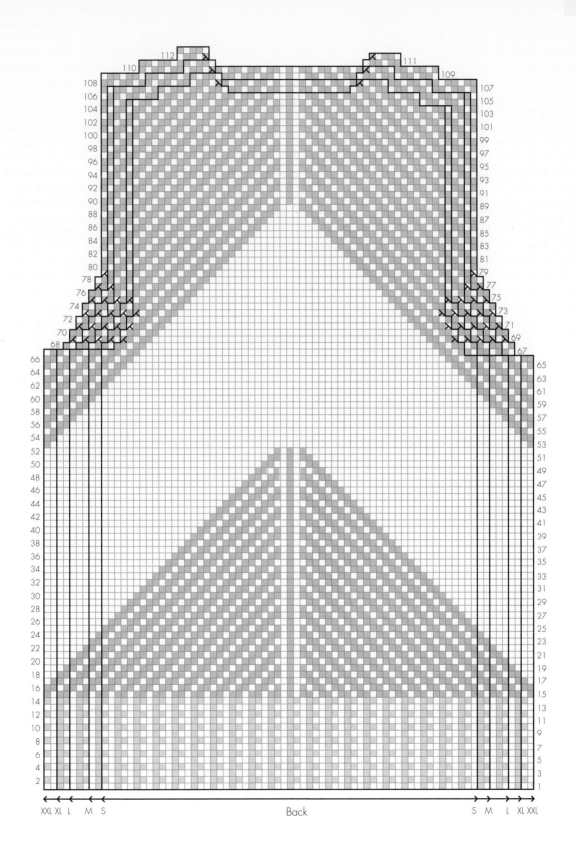

lace sweater

A ***whisper-fine silk and mohair*** yarn is perfect for this delicate lace sweater—the height of indulgence.

MATERIALS
Rowan Kidsilk Haze. Shade 590 Pearl. 14 (14, 15) x 25g balls (229 yds, 210m per ball). Use two strands of yarn throughout.

1 pair size 6 (4mm) needles.

GAUGE
2 patt repeats (18 sts) = 3¼" (8cm) wide using 2 strands of yarn on size 6 (4mm) needles, or needles required to obtain this gauge.

PATTERN
BACK
Cast on 111 (129, 147) sts.
Purl 1 row.

Work lace patt as follows:
Row 1 K2, * yo, k2, s1, k1, psso, k2tog, k2, yo, k1, repeat from * to last st, k1.
Row 2 Purl.
Row 3 K1, * yo, k2, s1, k1, psso, k2tog, k2, yo, k1, repeat from * to last 2 sts, k2.
Row 4 Purl.
These 4 rows form lace patt repeat.

Rows 5–12 Work rows 1–4 twice.
Work 8 rows in St st.
** Work 12 rows of lace patt as before, then 4 rows in St st.**
** to ** forms the patt repeat.
Cont in patt until back measures 13" (33cm).

SIZE		
SMALL–MEDIUM	MEDIUM–LARGE	LARGE–XL
To fit bust		
32–36" (81–91.5cm)	36–39" (91.5–99cm)	40–44" (102–112cm)
Actual size		
37" (94cm)	43" (109cm)	49" (124cm)
Back length		
22½" (57cm)	23" (58.5cm)	24" (61cm)
Sleeve seam		
19¼" (49cm)	19¼" (49cm)	19¼" (49cm)

GARMENT SIZING See page 124
ABBREVIATIONS See page 126

Shape armhole

Bind off 4 (8, 12) sts at beg of next 2 rows.
Dec 1 st at each end of next and every other row
until 93 (97, 103) sts remain.
Cont without shaping until work measures 21 (21½,
22½)" [53 (55, 57)cm], ending with a WS row.

Shape shoulders and neck

LEFT SIDE OF NECK
Bind off 5 sts at beg of next 6 rows.
Row 7 Bind off 5 sts, patt 13 (15, 17), bind off
27 (27, 29) sts, patt to end.
Working on 18 (20, 22) sts.
Row 8 Bind off 5 sts, patt to end.
Row 9 Bind off 3 sts, patt to end.
Row 10 Bind off 4 (5, 6) sts, patt to end.
Row 11 Bind off 2 sts, patt to end.
Row 12 Bind off rem sts.

RIGHT SIDE OF NECK
With WS facing, rejoin yarn to rem stitches at neck
edge and work rows 9–12.

FRONT

Work as for back to completion of armhole shaping
– 93 (97, 103) sts.

Shape neck

LEFT SIDE OF NECK
Patt 47 (49, 52), turn and cast on 1 st. Keeping
lace patt correct, cont on these sts until front measures
21 (21½, 22½)" [53 (55, 57)cm], ending with a
WS row.

Shape shoulder

Bind off 5 sts beg of next and foll 3 RS rows.
Work 1 row.
Bind off 4 (5, 6) sts at beg of next row.
Work 1 row.
Bind off 4 (5, 7) sts at beg of next row.
On 20 sts cont until extension fits halfway around
back neck. Bind off.

RIGHT SIDE OF NECK
With RS facing, rejoin yarn to rem sts at neck edge.
Cast on 2 sts. Work to match left side, reversing
all shaping.

SLEEVES

Cast on 66 (66, 75) sts. Purl 1 row.
Work 12 rows in lace patt, then 8 rows in St st.

Change to main garment repeat (** to **), inc 1 st
at each end of 3rd and every foll 16th row to 76
(82, 91) sts, working extra sts into patt.
Cont without shaping until work measures 19¼"
(49cm).

Shape sleeve cap

Bind off 4 (3, 4) sts at beg of next 2 (4, 4) rows.
Dec 1 st each end of next and every other row to 44
(44, 45) sts.
Work 1 row.
Dec 1 st at each end of next 4 rows.
Bind off 3 sts at beg of next 4 rows.
Bind off rem sts.

FINISHING

Weave in any loose ends. Join shoulder and side
seams. Join neck extensions and sew to back neck.
Join sleeve seams. Line up sleeve cap to armhole
and stitch. Press lightly using a warm iron over a
damp cloth.

shawl collar jacket

Relaxed and elegant, this softly draping cardigan is worked in a beautiful *kid mohair and silk* mix yarn.

MATERIALS
Rowan Kidsilk Haze. Shade 589 Majestic. 14 (14, 15, 15, 16) x 25g balls (229 yds, 210m per ball).

1 pair size 3 (3.25mm) and 1 pair size 6 (4mm) needles.

Stitch holder.

GAUGE
22 sts and 30 rows = 4 x 4" (10 x 10cm) over stockinette stitch using size 6 (4mm) needles and 2 strands of yarn, or needles required to obtain this gauge.

PATTERN
BACK
Cast on 112 (120, 128, 136, 144) sts using smaller needles and 2 strands of yarn.
Knit 4 rows.
Change to larger needles and St st.
Cont until work measures 15½" (39cm).

Shape armhole
Bind off 4 (5, 6, 7, 8) sts at beg of next 2 rows – 104 (110, 116, 122, 128) sts.
Row 3 K2, s1, k1, psso, knit to last 4 sts, k2tog, k2 – 102 (108, 114, 120, 126) sts.
Row 4 Purl.
Rows 5–12 Repeat rows 3 and 4 four times – 94 (100, 106, 112, 118) sts.
Work 54 (56, 58, 60, 62) more rows in St st.

SIZES				
SMALL	MEDIUM	LARGE	XL	XXL
To fit bust				
34–36" (86–91.5cm)	37–39" (94–99cm)	40–42" (102–107cm)	43–45" (109–114cm)	46–48" (117–122cm)
Actual size				
39" (99cm)	42½" (108cm)	45½" (116cm)	48" (122cm)	51½" (130cm)
Back length				
25" (63.5cm)	25" (63.5cm)	26" (66cm)	26½" (67cm)	27" (68cm)
Sleeve seam				
19" (48cm)	19" (48cm)	19" (48cm)	19" (48cm)	19" (48cm)

GARMENT SIZING See page 124
ABBREVIATIONS See page 126

Shape shoulders and neck

Rows 1–6 Bind off 5 sts beg each row – 64 (70, 76, 82, 88) sts.

Row 7 Bind off 5 sts, k13 (15, 17, 19, 21) including st on RH needle after bind off, bind off 28 (30, 32, 34, 36) sts, k18 (20, 22, 24, 26).

On last 18 (20, 22, 24, 26) sts.

Row 8 Bind off 5 sts, purl to last 2 sts, p2tog – 12 (14, 16, 18, 20) sts.

Row 9 K2tog, knit to end – 11 (13, 15, 17, 19) sts.

Row 10 Bind off 5 (6, 7, 8, 9) sts, purl to end – 6 (7, 8, 9, 10) sts.

Row 11 K2tog, knit to end – 5 (6, 7, 8, 9) sts. Bind off rem sts.

Rejoin yarn to rem sts at neck edge.

Row 8 P2tog, purl to end – 12 (14, 16, 18, 20) sts.

Row 9 Bind off 5 (6, 7, 8, 9) sts, knit to last 2 sts, K2tog – 6 (7, 8, 9, 10) sts.

Row 10 P2tog, purl to end – 5 (6, 7, 8, 9) sts. Bind off rem sts.

POCKET LININGS (make 2)

Cast on 22 sts using larger needles and 2 strands of yarn.

Work 7" (18cm) in garter stitch (every row, knit). Leave sts on holder.

LEFT FRONT

Cast on 64 (68, 72, 76, 80) sts using smaller needles and 2 strands of yarn.

Row 1 K44 (48, 52, 56, 60), *p2, k2, repeat from * to end.

Row 2 Knit.

Rows 3–4 Repeat rows 1 and 2.

Change to larger needles and work as folls.

Row 1 K44 (48, 52, 56, 60), *p2, k2, repeat from * to end.

Row 2 K20, p44 (48, 52, 56, 60).

Rep rows 1 and 2 until work measures 7" (18cm), ending with a row 2.

Place pocket

Next row (RS) K13 (15, 17, 19, 21), place next 22 sts on holder, knit across 22 sts of pocket lining, k9 (11, 13, 15, 17), *p2, k2, repeat from * to end – 64 (68, 72, 76, 80) sts.

Cont in St st with front broken rib border until work measures 15½" (39cm), ending with a WS row.

Shape armhole and shawl collar

Row 1 (RS) Bind off 4 (5, 6, 7, 8) sts, patt to end – 60 (63, 66, 69, 72) sts.

Row 2 Patt.

Row 3 K2, s1, k1, psso, k36 (39, 42, 45, 48), (p2, k2) four times, p1, inc, k2 – 60 (63, 66, 69, 72) sts.

Row 4 K2, p2, k17, purl to end.

Row 5 K2, s1, k1, psso, k35 (38, 41, 44, 47), (p2, k2) four times, p1, inc, k3 – 60 (63, 66, 69, 72) sts.

Row 6 K2, p2, k18, purl to end.

Row 7 K2, s1, k1, psso, k34 (37, 40, 43, 46), (p2, k2) four times, p1, inc, k4 – 60 (63, 66, 69, 72) sts.

Row 8 K2, p2, k19, purl to end.

Row 9 K2, s1, k1, psso, k33 (36, 39, 42, 45), (p2, k2) four times, p1, inc, k5 – 60 (63, 66, 69, 72) sts.

Row 10 K2, p2, k2, p1, k17, purl to end.

Row 11 K2, s1, k1, psso, k32 (35, 38, 41, 44), (p2, k2) four times, p1, inc, k6 – 60 (63, 66, 69, 72) sts.

Row 12 (K2, p2) twice, k17, purl to end.

Row 13 K35 (38, 41, 44, 47), (p2, k2) four times, p1, inc, k7 – 61 (64, 67, 70, 73) sts.

Row 14 (K2, p2) twice, k18, purl to end.

Row 15 K35 (38, 41, 44, 47), (p2, k2) four times, p1, inc, k8 – 62 (65, 68, 71, 74) sts.

Row 16 (K2, p2) twice, k19, purl to end.

Row 17 K35 (38, 41, 44, 47), (p2, k2) four times, p1, k10.

Row 18 (K2, p2) twice, k19, purl to end.
Row 19 K35 (38, 41, 44, 47), (p2, k2) four times,
p1, inc, k9 – 63 (66, 69, 72, 75) sts.
Row 20 (K2, p2) twice, k2, p1, k17, purl to end.

Keeping collar patt correct, cont as folls.
NOTE: Only the shaping rows are given.
Row 23 K35 (38, 41, 44, 47), (p2 , k2) four times,
p1, inc, k10 – 64 (67, 70, 73, 76) sts.
Row 24 (K2, p2) three times, k16, k2tog, purl to
end – 63 (66, 69, 72, 75) sts.
Row 27 K34 (37, 40, 43, 46), (p2, k2) four times,
p1, inc, k11 – 64 (67, 70, 73, 76) sts.
Row 31 K34 (37, 40, 43, 46), (p2, k2) four times,
p1, inc, k12 – 65 (68, 71, 74, 77) sts.
Row 34 (K2, p2) three times, k18, k2tog, purl to
end – 64 (67, 70, 73, 76) sts.
Row 35 K33 (36, 39, 42, 45), (p2, k2) four times,
p1, inc, k13 – 65 (68, 71, 74, 77) sts.
Row 39 K33 (36, 39, 42, 45), (p2, k2) four times,
p1, inc, k14 – 66 (69, 72, 75, 78) sts.
Row 43 K33 (36, 39, 42, 45), (p2, k2) four times,
p1, inc, k15 – 67 (70, 73, 76, 79) sts.
Row 44 (K2, p2) four times, k17, k2tog, purl to end
– 66 (69, 72, 75, 78) sts.
Row 47 K32 (35, 38, 41, 44), (p2, k2) four times,
p1, inc, k16 – 67 (70, 73, 76, 79) sts.
Row 51 K32 (35, 38, 41, 44), (p2, k2) four times,
p1, inc, k17 – 68 (71, 74, 77, 80) sts.
Row 54 (K2, p2) four times, k2, p1, k16, k2tog,
purl to end – 67 (70, 73, 76, 79) sts.
Row 55 K31 (34, 37, 40, 43), (p2, k2) four times,
p1, inc, k18 – 68 (71, 74, 77, 80) sts.
Row 64 (K2, p2) five times, k16, k2tog, purl to end
– 67 (70, 73, 76, 79) sts.
Work 2 (4, 6, 8, 10) more rows in patt.

Shape shoulders

Keeping collar section patts correct, bind off 5 sts
at beg next and foll 2 RS rows – 52 (55, 58, 61,
64) sts.
Work 1 row.
Bind off 5 (6, 7, 8, 9) sts at beg next and foll 2 RS
rows – 37 sts.

Keeping patts correct, cont until extension fits around half of the back neck.
Bind off.

RIGHT FRONT

Cast on 64 (68, 72, 76, 80) sts using smaller needles and 2 strands of yarn.

Row 1 (K2, p2) five times, k44 (48, 52, 56, 60).
Row 2 Knit.
Rows 3–4 Repeat rows 1 and 2.

Change to larger needles and work as folls.
Row 1 (K2, p2) five times, k44 (48, 52, 56, 60).
Row 2 P44 (48, 52, 56, 60), k20.
Rep rows 1 and 2 until work measures 7" (18cm), ending with a row 2.

Place pocket

Next row (RS) (K2, p2) five times, k9 (11, 13, 15, 17), place next 22 sts on holder, knit across 22 sts of pocket lining, knit to end – 64 (68, 72, 76, 80) sts.
Cont in St st with front broken rib border until work measures 15½" (39cm), ending with a RS row.

Shape armhole and shawl collar

Row 1 (WS) Bind off 4 (5, 6, 7, 8) sts, patt to end – 60 (63, 66, 69, 72) sts.
Row 2 K2, inc, p1, (k2, p2) four times, knit to last 4 sts, k2tog, k2 – 60 (63, 66, 69, 72) sts.
Row 3 P39 (42, 45, 48, 51), k17, p2, k2.
Row 4 K3, inc, p1, (k2, p2) four times, knit to last 4 sts, k2tog k2 – 60 (63, 66, 69, 72) sts.
Row 5 P38 (41, 44, 47, 50), k18, p2, k2.
Row 6 K4, inc, p1, (k2, p2) four times, knit to last 4 sts, k2tog, k2 – 60 (63, 66, 69, 72) sts.
Row 7 P37 (40, 43, 46, 49), k19, p2, k2.
Row 8 K5, inc, p1, (k2, p2) four times, knit to last 4 sts, k2tog, k2 – 60 (63, 66, 69, 72) sts.
Row 9 P36 (39, 42, 45, 48), k17, p1, k2, p2, k2.
Row 10 K6, inc, p1, (k2, p2) four times, knit to last 4 sts, k2tog, k2 – 60 (63, 66, 69, 72) sts.
Row 11 P35 (38, 41, 44, 47), k17, (p2, k2) twice.

Row 12 K7, inc, p1, (k2, p2) four times, knit to end – 61 (64, 67, 70, 73) sts.

Row 13 P35 (38, 41, 44, 47), k18, (p2, k2) twice.

Row 14 K8, inc, p1, (k2, p2) four times, knit to end – 62 (65, 68, 71, 74) sts.

Row 15 P35 (38, 41, 44, 47), k19, (p2, k2) twice.

Row 16 K10, p1, (k2, p2) four times, knit to end.

Row 17 P35 (38, 41, 44, 47), k19, (p2, k2) twice.

Row 18 K9, inc, p1, (k2, p2) four times, knit to end – 63 (66, 69, 72, 76) sts.

Row 19 P35 (38, 41, 44, 47), k17, p1, k2, (p2, k2) twice.

Keeping collar patt correct, cont as folls.
NOTE: Only the shaping rows are given.

Row 22 K10, inc, p1, (k2, p2) four times, knit to end – 64 (67, 70, 73, 76) sts.

Row 23 P34 (37, 40, 43, 46), k2tog, k16, (p2, k2) three times – 63 (66, 69, 72, 75) sts.

Row 26 K11, inc, p1, (k2, p2) four times, knit to end – 64 (67, 70, 73, 76) sts.

Row 30 K12, inc, p1, (k2, p2) four times, knit to end – 65 (68, 71, 74, 77) sts.

Row 33 P33 (36, 39, 42, 45), k2tog, k16, k2, (p2, k2) three times – 64 (67, 70, 73, 76) sts.

Row 34 K13, inc, p1, (k2, p2) four times, knit to end – 65 (68, 71, 74, 77) sts.

Row 38 K14, inc, p1, (k2, p2) four times, knit to end – 66 (69, 72, 75, 78) sts.

Row 42 K15, inc, p1, (k2, p2) four times, knit to end – 67 (70, 73, 76, 79) sts.

Row 43 P32 (35, 38, 41, 44), k2tog, k16, k1, (p2, k2) four times – 66 (69, 72, 75, 78) sts.

Row 46 K16, inc, p1, (k2, p2) four times, knit to end – 67 (70, 73, 76, 79) sts.

Row 50 K17, inc, p1, (k2, p2) four times, knit to end – 68 (71, 74, 77, 79) sts.

Row 53 P31 (34, 37, 40, 43), k2tog, k16, p1, k2, (p2, k2) four times – 67 (70, 73, 76, 79) sts.

Row 54 18, inc, p1, (k2, p2) four times, knit to end – 68 (71, 74, 77, 79) sts.

Row 63 P30 (33, 36, 39, 42), k2tog, k16, p2, k2, (p2, k2) four times – 67 (70, 73, 76, 79) sts.
Work 3 (5, 7, 9, 11) more rows.

Shape shoulders

Keeping collar section patts correct, bind off 5 sts beg next and foll 2 WS rows – 52 (55, 58, 61, 64) sts.
Work 1 row.
Bind off 5 (6, 7, 8, 9) sts beg next and foll 2 WS rows – 37 sts.
Keeping patts correct, cont until extension fits across half of the back neck.
Bind off.

SLEEVES

Cast on 56 (58, 60, 62, 64) sts using smaller needles and 2 strands of yarn.
Knit 4 rows.
Change to larger needles and St st.
Inc 1 st at each end of row 11 and every foll 12th row to 72 (76, 80, 82, 84) sts.
Cont without shaping until work measures 19" (48cm).

Shape sleeve cap

Bind off 4 (5, 6) sts at beg of next 2 rows.
Row 3 K2, s1, k1, psso, knit to last 4 sts, k2tog, k2.
Row 4 Purl.
Rep rows 3 and 4 until 30 sts rem.
Dec 1 st at each end of next 4 rows – 22 sts.
Bind off.

POCKET TOPS

With RS facing and using smaller needles and 2 strands of yarn, knit 4 rows across pocket sts on holder. Bind off.

FINISHING

Weave in any loose ends. Join extension bind-off edges, remembering that the collar folds over to the outside. Join shoulder and neckband seams. Join side and sleeve seams. Ease sleeve cap into armhole and stitch. Slipstitch pockets and pocket tops into place. Press lightly using a warm iron over a damp cloth.

CHAPTER 3

from day to evening

These rich and special day-to-evening pieces include sensuous camisoles, fine detailed sweaters, cardigans, and tops. Delicate, whisper-fine mohair and merino wool fabrics combine with lace, beading, and decorative touches of silk and satin ribbons. Beautiful garment shapes are enhanced by special trims and decorative details in sumptuous yarns and colors.

crossover cardigan

This stylish wraparound cardigan, worked in *softest silk and kid mohair* yarn, is a timeless piece for any occasion.

MATERIALS
Rowan Kidsilk Haze. Shade 600 Dewberry. 12 (13, 13) x 25g balls (229 yds, 210m per ball).

1 pair size 6 (4mm) and 1 pair size 8 (5mm) needles.

2 knitting markers.

GAUGE
20 sts and 24 rows = 4 x 4" (10 x 10cm) over stockinette stitch and 2 ends of yarn on size 8 (5mm) needles, or needles required to obtain this gauge.

PATTERN
BACK
Cast on 88 (96, 104) sts using smaller needles and 2 strands of yarn.
Row 1 (RS) * K2, p1, k1, repeat from * to end.
Row 2 * K1, p3, repeat from * to end.
These 2 rows form seed stitch rib patt.
Cont in patt until back measures 2½" (6cm), ending with a row 2.**
Change to larger needles and work 46 (48, 50) rows in St st, beg with a knit row.

Shape armhole
Bind off 4 (5, 6) sts at beg of next 2 rows.
Row 3 K2, s1, k1, psso, knit to last 4 sts, k2tog, k2.

SIZE		
SMALL	MEDIUM	LARGE
To fit bust		
32–34" (81–86cm)	34–36" (86–91cm)	37–39" (94–99cm)
Actual size		
36" (91.5cm)	37" (94cm)	40" (102cm)
Back length		
19½" (49.5cm)	20" (51cm)	20½" (52cm)
Sleeve seam		
19" (48cm)	19" (48cm)	19" (48cm)

GARMENT SIZING See page 124
ABBREVIATIONS See page 126

Row 3 Knit.
Row 4 Bind off 3 sts, purl to end.
Row 5 Knit.
Row 6 Bind off 2 sts, purl to end.
Row 7 Knit to last 4 sts, k2tog, k2.
Row 8 P2, p2tog, purl to end.
Repeat rows 7 and 8 until completion of 24th (30th, 36th) row – 61 (63, 65) sts.
Change dec to RS rows (every other row) only and cont to completion of 46th (48th, 50th) row – 50 (54, 58) sts.

Shape armhole
Row 1 (RS) Bind off 4 (5, 6) sts, knit to last 4 sts, k2tog, k2.
Row 2 Purl.
Row 3 K2, s1, k1, psso, knit to last 4 sts, k2tog, k2.
Row 4 Purl.
Repeat rows 3 and 4 until 37 (38, 39) sts remain.
Cont dec at neck edge only until 18 (19, 20) sts remain, ending with a RS row.
Work 3 rows.

Shape shoulder
RS facing. Bind off 3 sts at beg of next and 4 foll RS rows.
Work 1 row.
Bind off.

RIGHT FRONT
Work as for left front but reverse shaping by:
Row 1 Bind off 4 sts, knit to end.
Row 2 Purl.
Row 3 Bind off 3 sts, knit to end.
Row 4 Purl.
Row 5 Bind off 2 sts, knit to end.
Row 6 Purl.
Row 7 K2, s1, k1, psso, knit to end.
Row 8 Purl to last 4 sts, p2tog tbl, p2.

SLEEVES
Cast on 50 (52, 54) sts using smaller needles and 2 strands of yarn.

Row 4 Purl.
Repeat rows 3 and 4 until 72 (76, 80) sts remain, ending with a purl row.
Work 40 rows in St st without shaping.

Shape shoulders and neck
Rows 1–6 Bind off 3 sts, work to end.
Row 7 Bind off 3 sts, k11 (12, 13), bind off 26 (28, 30) sts, work to end.

LEFT SIDE OF NECK
Rows 8–10 Bind off 3 sts, work to end.
Row 11 Bind off 2 sts, work to end.
(MEDIUM AND LARGE SIZES ONLY)
Row 12 Bind off rem sts.

RIGHT SIDE OF NECK
WS facing, rejoin yarn to rem sts at neck edge and work rows 9–12.

LEFT FRONT
Work as back to **.
Change to larger needles and St st.
Row 1 Knit.
Row 2 Bind off 4 sts, purl to end.

Work ¾" (2cm) in seed stitch as established for
the back.

Change to larger needles and St st, beginning with
a knit row.
Inc 1 st at each end of 11th row and every foll 12th
row to 64 (66, 68) sts.
Cont without shaping until sleeve measures 19"
(48cm).

Shape sleeve cap
Rows 1 and 2 Bind off 4 (5, 6) sts, work to end.
Row 3 K2, s1, k1, psso, knit to last 4 sts, k2tog,
k2.
Row 4 Purl.
Repeat rows 3 and 4 until 30 (28, 26) sts remain,
ending with a row 4.
Bind off.

FINISHING
Join shoulder seams.

Ties and Front band
Cast on 5 sts using smaller needles and 2 strands
of yarn.
Work 16" (40cm) in seed stitch as established for the
back. Place marker at end of last row. Cont in seed
stitch until band fits, from marker, around front edge
of garment, starting and finishing above the seed
stitch rib. Place second marker. Work a further 27½"
(70cm) in seed stitch.
Bind off.

Attach band: Marker 1 to right front at top of rib,
marker 2 to left front at top of rib. Sew band around
front of cardigan.

Join side seams, leaving 1¼" (3cm) gap above rib in
right side seam. Join sleeve seams. Line up sleeve
cap to armhole and sew. Press lightly using a warm
iron over a damp cloth.

beaded sweater

Exquisite, staggered bead detailing enhances this luxurious *extra-fine merino* sweater. This is the perfect piece for a special daytime or evening occasion.

MATERIALS

Rowan 4 ply Soft. Shade 386 Irish Cream. 7 (8, 8) x 50g balls (191 yds, 175m per ball).

1 pair size 2 (2.75mm) and 1 pair size 3 (3.25mm) needles.

4,000 beads, approx. 1.5mm in diameter

GAUGE

28 sts and 36 rows = 4 x 4" (10 x 10cm) over stockinette stitch on size 3 (3.25mm) needles, or needles required to obtain this gauge.

PATTERN
BACK

Cast on 127 (139, 151) sts using smaller needles.
Work in garter rib as folls.
Row 1 Knit.
Row 2 *P1, k2, repeat from * to last st, k1.
Rows 3–8 Repeat rows 1 and 2 three times, inc 1 st at end of last row – 128 (140, 152) sts.
Change to larger needles and St st. Cont until work measures 5" (12cm).

SIZES		
SMALL	MEDIUM	LARGE
To fit bust		
34" (86cm)	36" (91.5cm)	38" (96.5cm)
Actual size		
36" (91.5cm)	39" (99cm)	42½" (108cm)
Back length		
23¼" (59cm)	23½" (60cm)	23¾" (60.5cm)
Sleeve seam		
13" (33cm)	13" (33cm)	13" (33cm)

GARMENT SIZING See page 124
ABBREVIATIONS See page 126
SPECIAL ABBREVIATION PB = Wyif slip the next 2 sts purlwise, place 2 beads next to right hand needle, then take yarn back.

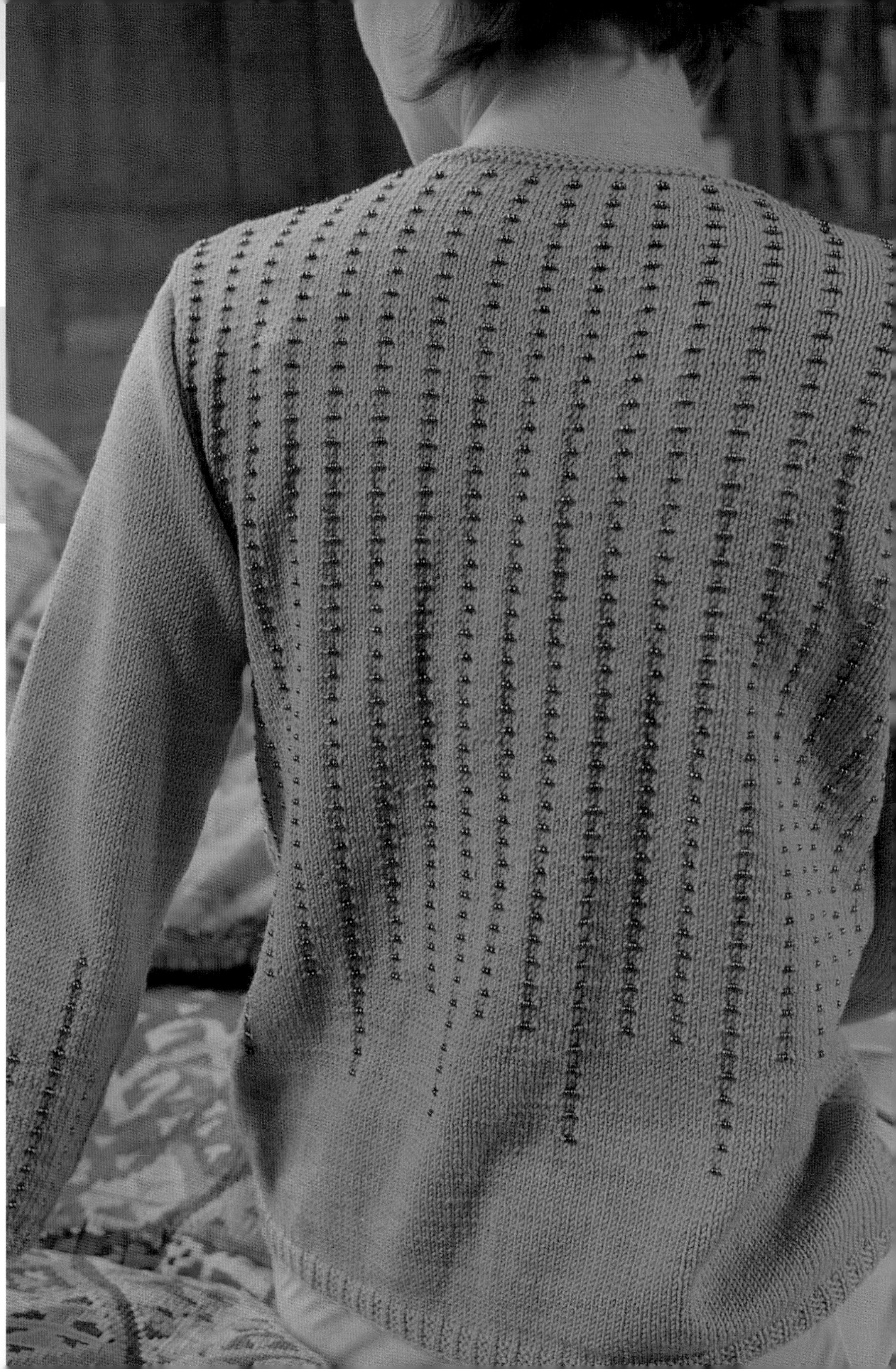

Change to bead patt 1 as folls.

Thread approx. 500 beads onto ball of yarn.

Row 1 K18 (6, 12), (PB, k16) five (seven, seven) times, PB, k18 (6,12).

Row 2 Purl.

Row 3 Knit.

Row 4 Purl.

Rows 5–20 Repeat rows 1–4 four times.

Change to bead patt 2 as folls.

Row 1 K6, *PB, k4, repeat from * to last 8 sts, PB, k6.

Row 2 Purl.

Row 3 Knit.

Row 4 Purl.

Rows 1–4 form bead patt 2.

Cont in bead patt 2 until work measures 15" (38cm).

Shape armhole

Keeping patt correct, bind off 4 (5, 6) sts beg next 2 rows – 120 (130, 140) sts.

Dec 1 st at each end of next and every other row until 112 (120,128) sts rem.**

Cont without shaping until work measures 22¾ (23, 23¼)" [58 (58.5, 59)cm].

Shape shoulders and neck

Rows 1–4 Bind off 6 (6, 7) sts, patt to end – 88 (96, 100) sts.

Row 5 Bind off 6 (6, 7) sts, patt 21 (24, 24), including st already on RH needle after bind off, bind off 34 (36, 38) sts, patt 27 (30, 31).

On 27 (30, 31) sts.

Row 6 Bind off 6 (6, 7) sts, patt to end – 21 (24, 24) sts.

Row 7 Bind off 5 sts, patt to end – 16 (19, 19) sts.

Row 8 Bind off 6 (7, 7) sts, patt to end – 10 (12, 12) sts.

Row 9 Bind off 5 sts, patt to end – 5 (7, 7) sts.

Bind off.

Rejoin yarn to rem 21 (24, 24) sts at neck edge and work rows 7–10.

FRONT

Work as for back until completion of armhole shaping at ** – 112 (120, 128) sts.

Divide for front opening

RS facing, patt 56 (60, 64) sts, turn and work on these sts.

Keeping bead patt correct, work k2 at neck edge on every row.

Cont until work measures approx 20 (20½, 21)" [51 (52, 53)cm], ending with row 3.

Shape neck

Next row (WS) Bind off 11 (12, 13) sts, patt to end – 45 (48, 51) sts.

Dec 1 st at neck edge on next 8 rows – 37 (40, 43) sts.

Dec 1 st at neck edge on next and every other row until 29 (32, 35) sts rem.

Cont without shaping until work measures same as back at shoulder, ending with a purl row.

Shape shoulder

Bind off 6 (6, 7) sts at beg of next and foll 2 alt rows – 11 (14, 14) sts.

Work 1 row.

Bind off 6 (7, 7) sts at beg of next row – 5 (7, 7) sts.

Work 1 row.

Bind off.

Rejoin yarn to rem sts at neck edge and work to match reversing all shaping.

SLEEVES

For each sleeve, thread approx. 250 beads onto ball of yarn.

Cast on 70 (70, 73) sts using smaller needles.

Work 8 rows in garter rib as for back.

MEDIUM SIZE Inc 1 st at each end of last row – 72 sts.

LARGE SIZE Inc 1 st at end of last row – 74 sts.

Change to larger needles and work 40 rows in bead patt 2, inc 1 st at each end of rows 11, 23, and 35, working extra sts into patt.

Row 1 Row 1 of bead patt 2 for sleeve (RS) K4 (5, 6) *PB, k4, repeat from* to last 6 (7, 8) sts, PB, k4 (5, 6).

Change to bead patt 1 and work 20 rows, inc 1 st at each end of row 47 and 59.

Row 41 Row 1 of bead patt 1 for sleeve (RS) K1 (2, 3), *PB, k16, repeat from * to last 3 (4, 5) sts, PB, k1 (2, 3).

Change to St st and cont inc 1 st at each end of every 10th row to 88 (90, 92) sts.

Cont without shaping until work measures 13" (33cm).

Shape sleeve cap

Bind off 4 (5, 6) sts beg next 2 rows – 80 (80, 80) sts.

Dec 1 st at each end of next 6 rows – 68 sts.

Dec 1 st at each end of next and every other row until 40 sts rem.

Work 1 row.

Dec 1 st at each end of next 4 rows – 32 sts.

Bind off.

NECK TRIM

Join shoulder seams.

With RS facing and using smaller needles, pick up and knit 35 (36, 37) sts from right front neck, 54 (56, 58) sts from back neck, and 35 (36, 37) sts from left front neck – 124 (128, 132) sts.

Knit 4 rows.

Bind off.

FINISHING

Weave in any loose ends. Join side and sleeve seams. Ease sleeve cap into armhole and stitch. Press lightly on WS using a warm iron over a damp cloth.

wide-neck lace sweater

This lavish lace sweater with an elegant scoop neck is worked in a combination of *finest silk and mohair* yarn in beautifully blended colors for a truly indulgent experience.

MATERIALS
Rowan Kidsilk Haze. Shades 595 Liqueur and 606 Candy Girl. 9 (9, 9, 10, 10) x 25g balls (229 yds, 210m per ball) in each color. Use two strands of yarn (one of each color) throughout.

1 pair size 3 (3.25mm) and 1 pair size 6 (4mm) needles.

GAUGE
2 patt repeats (20 sts) = 3½" (9cm) wide using 2 strands of yarn on size 6 (4mm) needles, or needles required to obtain this gauge.

PATTERN
BACK
Cast on 104 (112, 124, 132, 144) sts using smaller needles and 2 strands of yarn.
Work 6 rows in k2, p2 rib.
SMALL, LARGE, AND XX LARGE SIZES Dec 1 st at beg of last row − 103 (123, 143) sts.
MEDIUM AND EXTRA LARGE SIZES Inc 1 st at beg of last row − 113 (133) sts.

Change to larger needles and lace patt as follows.
Row 1 (RS) * K3, p1, yo, s1, k1, psso, k1, k2tog, yo, p1, repeat from * to last 3 sts, k3.
Row 2 * P3, k1, p5, k1, repeat from * to last 3 sts, p3.

SIZES				
SMALL	MEDIUM	LARGE	XL	XXL
To fit bust				
32–33"	34–36"	37–40"	41–42"	43–46"
(81–84cm)	(86–91.5cm)	(94–102cm)	(104–107cm)	(109–117cm)
Actual size				
35" (89cm)	38½" (98cm)	42" (107cm)	45½" (116cm)	49" (124cm)
Back length				
21½" (55cm)	22" (56cm)	22½" (57cm)	22¾" (58cm)	23½" (60cm)
Sleeve seam				
19¼" (49cm)	19¼" (49cm)	19¼" (49cm)	19¼" (49cm)	19¼" (49cm)

GARMENT SIZING See page 124
ABBREVIATIONS See page 126

Row 3 * K3, p1, k1, yo, s1, k2tog, psso, yo, k1, p1, repeat from * to last 3 sts, k3.

Row 4 * P3, k1, p5, k1, repeat from * to last 3 sts, p3.

These 4 rows form lace patt repeat. Cont in patt until work measures 13¾" (35cm).

Shape armhole

Bind off 3 (4, 5, 6, 7) sts at beg of next 2 rows.

Dec 1 st at each end of next and every other row until 91 (97, 103, 107, 111) sts remain. Cont without shaping until work measures 20½ (21, 21¼, 21½, 22)" [52 (53, 54, 55, 56)cm].

Shape neck

Row 1 Patt 29 (31, 33, 34, 35), bind off 33 (35, 37, 39, 41) sts, patt 29 (31, 33, 34, 35).

Work on these 29 (31, 33, 34, 35) sts for first side of neck.

Row 2 Patt.

Row 3 Bind off 5 sts, patt to end.

Rows 4–9 Repeat rows 2 and 3 three times – 9 (11, 13, 14, 15) sts.

Row 10 Patt.

Row 11 Bind off.

Second side of neck

Rejoin yarn to rem sts at neck edge and work rows 3 to 11 as given for first side of neck.

FRONT

Work as for back until front measures 18½ (19, 19¼, 19½, 20)" [47 (48, 49, 49.5, 51)cm].

Shape neck

Row 1 Patt 34 (36, 38, 39, 40), bind off 23 (25, 27, 29, 31) sts, patt 34 (36, 38, 39, 40).
Work on these 34 (36, 38, 39, 40) sts for first side of neck.
Row 2 Patt.
Row 3 Bind off 3 sts, patt to end.
Rows 4–11 Repeat rows 2 and 3 four times – 19 (21, 23, 24, 25) sts.
Row 12 Patt.
Row 13 Bind off 2 sts, patt to end.
Rows 14–21 Repeat rows 12 and 13 four times – 9 (11, 13, 14, 15) sts.
Row 22 Bind off.

SECOND SIDE OF NECK

Rejoin yarn to rem sts at neck edge and work rows 3–22 as given for first side of neck.

SLEEVES

Cast on 56 (56, 60, 60, 64) sts using smaller needles and 2 strands of yarn.
Work 6 rows in k2 p2 rib, inc 1 st at beg of last row – 57 (57, 61, 61, 65) sts.

Change to larger needles and lace patt, setting the position of the lace pattern as follows:
Row 1 K0 (0, 2, 2, 4), * p1, yo, s1, k1, psso, k1, k2tog, yo, p1, k3, repeat from *, ending last repeat k0 (0, 2, 2, 4) instead of k3.
Cont in patt, inc 1 st at each end of 11th row and every foll 14th (10th, 10th, 8th, 8th) row to 69 (75, 79, 85, 89) sts, working extra sts into patt.
Cont without shaping until work measures 19¼" (49cm).

Shape sleeve cap

Bind off 3 (4, 5, 6, 7) sts at beg of next 2 rows.
Dec 1 st at each end of next and every other row until 43 (45, 45, 47, 47) sts rem.
Work 1 row.
Dec 1 st at each end of next 4 rows.
Bind off 3 sts at beg of next 2 rows.
Bind off.

NECKBAND

Join right shoulder seam.
With RS facing, using smaller needles and 2 strands of yarn pick up and knit 26 sts from left side of front neck, 22 (24, 26, 28, 30) sts from center front neck, 25 sts from right side of front neck, 20 sts from right side of back neck, 32 (34, 36, 38, 40) sts from center back neck, and 20 sts from left side of back neck – 145 (149, 153, 157, 161) sts.
Work as follows:
Row 1 K1, *k2, p2, rep from * to end.
Row 2 * K2, p2, repeat from * to last stitch, k1.
Rows 3 and 4 Repeat rows 1 and 2.
Row 5 Repeat row 1.
Bind off in rib.

FINISHING

Weave in any loose ends. Join left shoulder and neckband seam. Join side and sleeve seams. Line up sleeve cap to armhole and stitch. Press lightly using a warm iron over a damp cloth.

beaded bolero

The elegance of this delightful beaded bolero speaks for itself—worked in an *extra-fine merino* yarn, this garment is sure to be treasured as an heirloom piece.

MATERIALS
Rowan 4ply Soft. Shade 387 Rain Cloud. 6 (7, 7, 8, 8) x 50g balls (191 yds, 175m per ball).

1 pair size 2 (2.75mm) and 1 pair size 3 (3.25mm) needles.

1 size 2 (2.75mm) circular needle.

4,500 beads, approx. 1.5mm in diameter.

GAUGE
28 sts and 36 rows = 4 x 4" (10 x 10cm) over stockinette stitch on size 3 (3.25mm) needles, or needles required to obtain this gauge.

NOTES
Thread 650 beads onto each ball of yarn. When knitting this design, omit bead if its position is an edge stitch.

SIZES

SMALL	MEDIUM	LARGE	XL	XXL
To fit bust				
34" (86cm)	36" (91.5cm)	38" (96.5cm)	40" (102cm)	42" (107cm)
Actual size				
35½" (90cm)	38" (96.5cm)	40" (102cm)	42" (107cm)	44½" (113cm)
Back length				
14½" (37cm)	14½" (37cm)	15" (38cm)	15" (38cm)	15½" (39cm)
Sleeve seam				
19" (48cm)	19" (48cm)	19" (48cm)	19" (48cm)	19" (48cm)

GARMENT SIZING See page 124
ABBREVIATIONS See page 126
SPECIAL ABBREVIATION PB = Wyif slip the next st purlwise, place 1 bead next to right hand needle, then take yarn back.

PATTERN

BACK

Cast on 127 (135, 143, 151, 159) sts using smaller needles.

Work in beaded rib as folls.

Foundation row (WS) *P1, k1, repeat from * to last st, p1.

Row 1 (RS) *K1, p1, k1, PB, repeat from * to last 3 sts, k1, p1, k1.

Row 2 *P1, k1, repeat from * to last st, p1.

Rows 3–10 Repeat rows 1 and 2 four times.

Change to larger needles.
Work main bead patt as folls.

Row 1 K3 (1, 5, 3, 1), *PB, k5, repeat from * to last 4 (2, 6, 4, 2) sts, PB, k3 (1, 5, 3, 1).

Rows 2–4 St st.

Row 5 K6 (4, 2, 6, 4), *PB, k5, repeat from * to last 7 (5, 3, 7, 5) sts, PB, k6 (4, 2, 6, 4).

Rows 6–8 St st.

These 8 rows form main bead patt repeat. Working in bead patt, follow rows 9–132 (134, 136, 138, 140) from Back chart.

RIGHT AND LEFT FRONTS

Cast on 27 (31, 35, 39, 43) sts using larger needles and, working in main bead patt, follow rows 1–129/130 (131/132, 133/134, 135/136, 137/138) from appropriate Front chart. Place marker at front edge of row 25 on both fronts.

SLEEVES

Cast on 67 (71, 71, 75, 75) sts using smaller needles and work in beaded rib as on back.
Change to larger needles and main bead patt as given for back, setting the position of the pattern as folls.

Row 1 K3 (2, 2, 1, 1), *PB, k5, repeat from * to last 4 (3, 3, 2, 2) sts, PB, k3 (2, 2, 1, 1).

Cont in patt, inc 1 st at each end of 11th and every foll 12th (12th, 10th, 10th, 8th) row to 83 (87, 91, 95, 99) sts, working extra sts into patt. Cont without shaping until work measures 19" (48cm).

Shape sleeve cap
Bind off 5 (6, 7, 8, 9) sts at beg next 2 rows – 73 (75, 77, 79, 81) sts.
Dec 1 st at each end of next and every other row to 49 sts.
Work 1 row.
Dec 1 st at each end of next and every foll 4th row to 43 sts.
Work 3 rows.
Bind off 4 sts beg next 2 rows – 35 sts.
Bind off.

FRONT BAND

Join shoulder and side seams.

Using the circular needle, with RS facing and starting at right side seam, pick up and knit 27 (31, 35, 39, 43) sts from right front cast on, 32 sts around shaping to row 25, 82 (85, 88, 91, 94) sts to shoulder, 45 (47, 49, 51, 53) from back neck, 82 (85, 88, 91, 94) sts from shoulder to row 25 of left front, 32 sts from shaping, and 27 (31, 35, 39, 43) from cast on – 327 (343, 359, 375, 391) sts.
Working back and forth (not circular), work the foundation row, then rows 1–10 of beaded rib patt as given for back.
Bind off in rib.

FINISHING

Join front band to back rib. Join sleeve seams. Ease sleeve cap into armhole and stitch. Weave in any loose ends. Press lightly on WS using a warm iron over a damp cloth.

Key

□ Knit on RS, purl on WS

⊡ PB (place bead)

◩ K2tog

◪ Sl, k1, psso

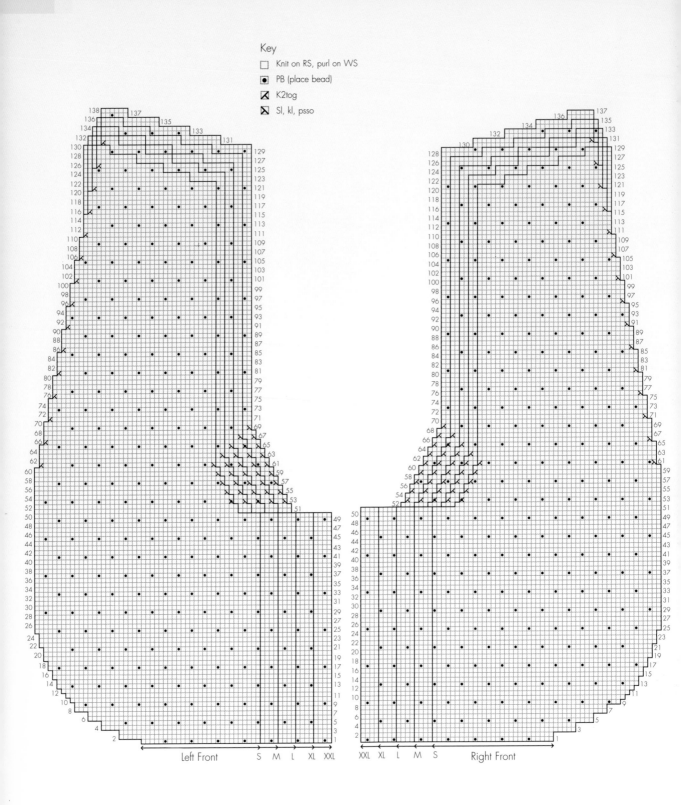

Left Front   S M L XL XXL   XXL XL L M S   Right Front

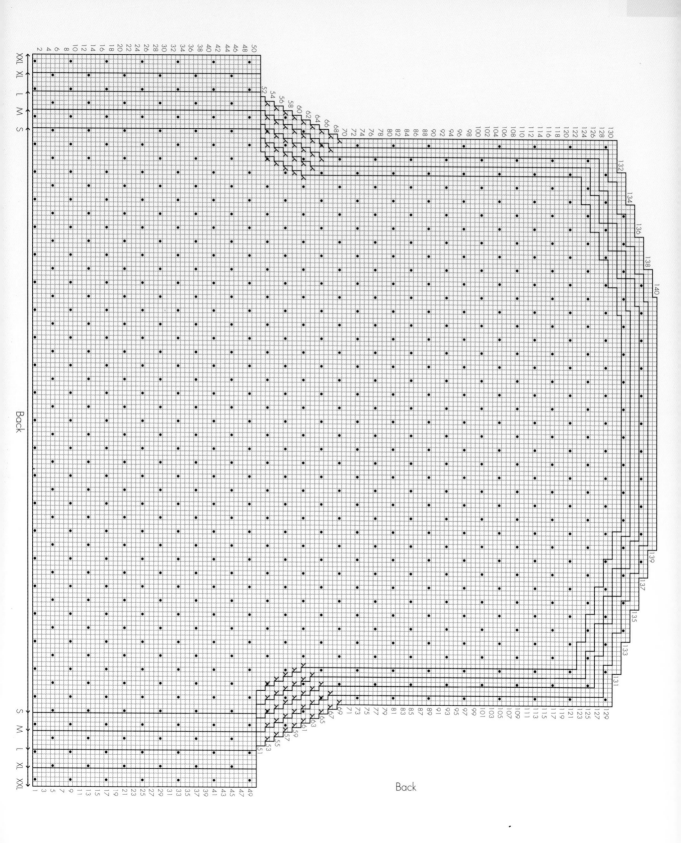

Back

Back

lace cardigan and camisole

Delicate lace patterning and fine drawstring detailing make this *fine merino* camisole and cardigan set a delightfully elegant combination.

SIZES		
SMALL	MEDIUM	LARGE
CARDIGAN		
To fit bust		
34"	36–38"	40"
(86cm)	(91.5–96.5cm)	(102cm)
Actual size		
36"	39"	42½"
(91.5cm)	(99cm)	(108cm)
Back length		
23"	23"	23"
(58.5cm)	(58.5cm)	(58.5cm)
Sleeve seam		
19"	19"	19"
(48cm)	(48cm)	(48cm)
CAMISOLE		
Actual size		
33"	35"	39"
(84cm)	(89cm)	(99cm)
Length		
23"	23"	23"
(58.5cm)	(58.5cm)	(58.5cm)

MATERIALS
Jaeger Matchmaker Merino 4 ply. Shade 701 Heather. 12 (13, 14) 50g balls, (200 yds, 183m) per ball.

1 pair size 3 (3.25mm) needles.

10 small buttons or 4.4 yds (4m) of satin ribbon.

GAUGE
28 sts and 36 rows = 4 x 4" (10 x 10cm) over stockinette stitch using size 3 (3.25mm) needles, or needles required to obtain this gauge.

GARMENT SIZING See page 124
ABBREVIATIONS See page 126

cardigan

PATTERN
BACK
Cast on 129 (137, 145) sts.

SMALL AND LARGE SIZES
Row 1 (RS) K1, *p1, k1, repeat from * to end.
Row 2 K1, *p1, k1, repeat from * to end.
Rows 3 and 4 Work as rows 1 and 2.
Row 5 K1, *yo, s1, k1, psso, k3, k2tog, yo, k1, repeat from * to end.
Row 6 Purl.
Row 7 K2, *yo, s1, k1, psso, k1, k2tog, yo, k3, repeat from * to last 7 sts, yo, s1, k1, psso, k1, k2tog, yo, k2.
Row 8 Purl.
Row 9 K3, *yo, s1, k2tog, psso, yo, k5, repeat from * to last 6 sts, yo, s1, k2tog, psso, yo, k3.
Row 10 Purl.
Rows 11–14 Work as rows 1–4.
Row 15 Work as row 9.
Rows 16, 18, and 20 Purl.
Row 17 Work as row 7.
Row 19 Work as row 5.
Rows 1–20 form the lace patt repeat.
Work these 20 rows three more times.

MEDIUM SIZE
Row 1 (RS) K1, *p1, k1, repeat from * to end.
Row 2 K1, *p1, k1, repeat from * to end.
Rows 3 and 4 Work as rows 1 and 2.
Row 5 K2, *k2tog, yo, k1, yo, s1, k1, psso, k3, repeat from * to last 7sts, k2tog, yo, k1, yo, sl, k1, psso, k2.
Row 6 Purl.
Row 7 K1, *k2tog, yo, k3, yo, s1, k1, psso, k1, repeat to end.
Row 8 Purl.
Row 9 K2tog, yo, *k5, yo, s1, k2tog, psso, yo, repeat from * to last 7 sts, k5, yo, s1, k1, psso.
Row 10 Purl.
Rows 11–14 Work as rows 1–4.
Row 15 Work as row 9.

Rows 16, 18, and 20 Purl.
Row 17 Work as row 7.
Row 19 Work as row 5.
Rows 1–20 form the lace patt repeat.
Work these 20 rows three more times.

ALL SIZES
Change to seed stitch.
Row 1 and every row K1, *p1, k1, rep from * to end.
Cont until work measures 14" (35.5cm).

Shape armholes
Bind off 6 (7, 8) sts at beg of next 2 rows – 117 (123, 129) sts.
Dec 1 st at each end of next and every other row until 107 (111, 115) sts rem.
Cont without shaping until work measures 22" (56cm), ending with a WS row.

Shape shoulders and neck
Rows 1 and 2 Bind off 6 sts, work to end.
Row 3 Bind off 6 sts, patt 21 (23, 25) including st already on RH needle after bind off, bind off 41 sts, patt 27 (29, 31).

On 27 (29, 31) sts.
Row 4 Bind off 6 sts, work to end – 21 (23, 25) sts.
Row 5 Bind off 5 sts, work to end – 16 (18, 20) sts.
Row 6 Bind off 6 (6, 7) sts, work to end – 10 (12, 13) sts.
Row 7 Bind off 5 sts, work to end – 5 (7, 8) sts.
Bind off rem sts.

Rejoin yarn to rem 21 (23, 25) sts at neck edge and work rows 5–8.

LEFT FRONT
Cast on 65 (69, 73) sts.
Work 80 rows in lace patt as for back.

Change to seed stitch with lace panel edging.

Rows 1–4 Seed stitch.
Row 5 Seed stitch to last 9 sts, lace patt row 5.
Row 6 P9, seed stitch to end.
Cont with 9 st lace panel and seed stitch main body until work measures 14" (35.5cm), ending with a WS row.

Shape armhole

Bind off 6 (7, 8) sts at beg of next row.
Dec 1 st at beg of next and every other row until 54 (56, 58) sts rem.
Cont without shaping until work measures 19¼" (49cm), ending with a RS row.

Shape neck

Row 1 (WS) Bind off 13 sts, work to end – 41 (43, 45) sts.
Dec 1 st at neck edge on next 10 rows – 31 (33, 35) sts.
Dec neck edge on next and every other row until 23 (25, 27) sts rem.
Work 1 row.

Shape shoulder

Bind off 6 sts beg next and foll RS row – 11 (13, 15) sts.
Work 1 row.
Bind off 6 (6, 7) sts beg next row – 5 (7, 8) sts.
Work 1 row.
Bind off rem sts.

RIGHT FRONT

Work to match left front reversing all shaping.

SLEEVES

Cast on 73 (81, 81) sts.
Work 80 rows in lace patt as for back.

Change to seed stitch.
Inc 1 st at each end of row 3 and every foll 8th (8th, 6th) row to 85 (91, 97) sts.
Cont without shaping until work measures 19" (48cm).

Shape sleeve cap

Bind off 6 (7, 8) sts at beg of next 2 rows – 73 (77, 81) sts.

Dec 1 st at each end of next and every other row until 53 (57, 61) sts rem.

Work 1 row.

Dec 1 st at each end of next and every foll 4th row until 45 (49, 53) sts rem.

Work 1 row.

Dec 1 st at each end of next 6 rows – 33 (37, 41) sts.

Bind off.

NECKBAND

Join shoulder seams.

With RS facing, pick up and knit 42 (42, 44) sts from right front neck, 61 sts from back neck and 42 (42, 44) sts from left front neck – 145 (145, 149) sts.

Row 1 K1, *p1, k1, repeat from * to end.

Row 2 K1, p1, yo, p2tog, k1, *p1, k1, repeat from * to end.

Rows 3 and 4 Work as row 1.

Bind off in seed stitch.

FINISHING

Weave in any loose ends. Join shoulder and side seams. Join sleeve seams. Ease sleeve cap into armhole and stitch into place. Attach buttons to left front, evenly spaced, using eyelets in lace panel for buttonholes, or thread 2.2 yds (2m) of satin ribbon through neck eyelets (*see photograph*).

camisole

PATTERN
BACK

Cast on 121 (129, 137) sts.

ALL SIZES

Work 80 rows in lace patt as for back, following the instructions for the SMALL AND LARGE SIZES.

Change to seed stitch and cont until work measures 15" (38cm).

Shape armhole

Bind off 9 (10, 11) sts beg next 2 rows – 103 (109, 115) sts.

Dec 1 st at each end of next 4 rows – 95 (101, 107) sts.

Dec 1 st at each end of next and every other row until 85 (91, 97) sts rem.**

Cont without shaping until work measures 18¼ (18½, 18¾)" [46.5 (47, 47.5)cm], ending with a WS row.

Shape neck

*** Patt 25 (27, 29) sts, bind off 35 (37, 39) sts, patt 25 (27, 29) including st on RH needle after bind off.

On 25 (27, 29) sts, dec 1 st at neck edge on next 5 (6, 7) rows – 20 (21, 22) sts.

Dec 1 st at neck edge on next and every other row until 14 (15, 16) sts rem.

Work 1 row.

Dec 1 st at neck edge on next and every foll 4th row until 11 (12, 13) sts rem.

Cont without shaping until work measures 21¾ (22, 22¼)" [55.5 (56, 56.5)cm].

Bind off. ***

FRONT

Work as for back to **.

Work 6 (8, 10) rows in seed stitch.

Shape neck

Work from *** to *** as for Back.

FINISHING

Weave in any loose ends. Join the side and shoulder seams. Press lightly using a warm iron over a damp cloth.

Optional: Thread 2.2 yds (2m) of satin ribbon through alternate lace holes on top edge of lace panel (*see photograph*).

CHAPTER 4

summer
sensations

Elegant, refined, clean lines combine with super
refined cottons, slubbed silks, and crisp cotton
silk to create a collection of easy, relaxed
pieces that are ideal for summer evenings and
hazy days. Beautiful sweaters, cotton camisoles
with lace and drawstring details, and fine lace
cardigans make for the ultimate in summer luxury.

scoop-neck sweater

Perfect for lovely, lazy summer days, this easy, classic, scoop-neck sweater is worked in a slubbed *silk and cotton* blended yarn.

MATERIALS
Rowan Summer Tweed. Shade 506
  Ghost. 7 (8, 8, 9) x 50g hanks
  (137 yds, 125m per ball).

1 pair size 6 (4mm) and 1 pair
  size 8 (5mm) needles.

Stitch holders.

GAUGE
16 sts and 23 rows = 4 x 4" (10 x
  10cm) over stockinette stitch using
  size 8 (5mm) needles, or needles
  required to obtain this gauge.

SIZES			
SMALL	MEDIUM	LARGE	XL
To fit bust			
34–36" (86–91.5cm)	36–40" (91.5–102cm)	40–44" (102–112cm)	44–46" (112–117cm)
Actual size			
41" (104cm)	44" (112cm)	47" (119.5cm)	50" (127cm)
Back length			
23½" (60cm)	23¾" (60.5cm)	24" (61cm)	24½" (62cm)
Sleeve seam			
18½" (47cm)	18½" (47cm)	18½" (47cm)	18½" (47cm)

GARMENT SIZING See page 124
ABBREVIATIONS See page 126

PATTERN

BACK

Cast on 84 (88, 96, 100) sts using smaller needles.
Work 2" (5cm) in k2, p2, rib.

Row 1 and every row *K2, p2, repeat from *
to end.

MEDIUM AND EXTRA LARGE SIZES ONLY Inc 1 st at each
end of last row – 84 (90, 96, 102) sts.

Change to larger needles and St st.

Cont until work measures 13¾" (35cm).

Shape armholes

Rows 1 and 2 Bind off 3 sts, work to end –
78 (84, 90, 96) sts.

Row 3 K2, p1, s1, k1, psso, knit to last 5 sts,
k2tog, p1, k2 – 76 (82, 88, 94) sts.

Row 4 P2, k1, purl to last 3 sts, k1, p2.

Repeat rows 3 and 4 until 68 (72, 76, 80) sts rem.
**

Work a further 24 rows in St st.

Shape neck

Row 1 (RS) K21 (22, 23, 24), turn and work on
these sts.

Row 2 Bind off 3 sts, purl to end – 18 (19, 20,
21) sts.

Row 3 Knit.

Row 4 Work as row 2 – 15 (16, 17, 18) sts.

Rows 5–8 Dec 1 st at neck edge – 11 (12, 13,
14) sts.

Row 9 Dec 1 st at neck edge – 10 (11, 12,
13) sts.

Row 10 Purl.

Rows 11–16 Work as rows 9 and 10 – 7 (8, 9,
10) sts.

Shape shoulder

Row 17 (RS) Bind off 4 (4, 5, 5) sts, knit to end –
3 (4, 4, 5) sts.

Row 18 Purl.

Bind off.

With RS facing, place 26 (28, 30, 32) sts on stitch
holder. Rejoin yarn to rem sts at neck edge and knit
to end. Work to match first side of neck, reversing
shaping.

FRONT

Work as for back to **.

Work 2 more rows without shaping.

Shape neck

Row 1 K26 (27, 28, 29), turn and work on
these sts.

Row 2 P2tog, purl to end – 25 (26, 27, 28) sts.

Row 3 Knit to last 2 sts, k2tog – 24 (25, 26,
27) sts.

Rows 4–7 Work as rows 2 and 3 twice – 20 (21,
22, 23) sts.

Row 8 Purl.

Row 9 Knit to last 2 sts, k2tog – 19 (20, 21,
22) sts.

Rows 10–29 Work as rows 8 and 9 ten times –
9 (10, 11, 12) sts.

Rows 30–32 Work in St st.

Rows 33–40 Work as rows 29–32 twice – 7 (8,
9, 10) sts.

Shape shoulder

Row 41 Bind off 4 (4, 5, 5) sts, knit to end – 3 (4,
4, 5) sts.

Row 42 Purl.

Bind off.

With RS facing, place 16 (18, 20, 22) sts on stitch
holder. Rejoin yarn to rem sts at neck edge and knit
to end. Work to match first side of neck, reversing
shaping.

SLEEVES

Cast on 32 (32, 36, 36) sts using smaller needles.
Work 2" (5cm) in rib as for back.

MEDIUM AND EXTRA LARGE SIZES ONLY Inc 1 st at each
end of last row – 32 (34, 36, 38) sts.

Change to larger needles and St st.
Inc 1 st at each end of 5th and every foll
8th row to 54 (56, 58, 60) sts.
Cont without shaping until work measures
18½" (47cm).

Shape sleeve cap
Rows 1 and 2 Bind off 3 sts, work to end
– 48 (50, 52, 54) sts.
Row 3 K2, p1, s1, k1, psso, knit to last
5 sts, k2tog, p1, k2 – 46 (48, 50, 52) sts.
Row 4 P2, k1, purl to last 3 sts, k1, p2.
Repeat rows 3 and 4 until 28 sts rem.
Dec 1 st at each end of next 4 rows –
20 sts.
Bind off.

NECKBAND
Join right shoulder seam.
With RS facing and using smaller needles,
pick up and knit 40 sts from left side of front
neck, knit across 16 (18, 20, 22) front
neck sts on holder, pick up and knit 40 sts
from right side of front neck and 19 sts from
right side of back neck, knit across 26 (28,
30, 32) back neck sts on holder, and pick
up and knit 19 sts from left side of back
neck – 160 (164, 168, 172) sts.
Work 2" (5cm) in k2, p2 rib as for back.
Bind off in rib.

FINISHING
Weave in any loose ends. Join neckband
and left shoulder seam. Join side and sleeve
seams. Ease sleeve cap into armhole and
stitch. Press lightly using a warm iron over a
damp cloth.

ribbon-trim camisole

This beautiful, fitted *fine cotton* camisole is enhanced by decorative lace stitching. Thread *silk* ribbon through the lace as a drawstring for a delicate finishing touch.

MATERIALS
Jaeger Siena 4 ply. Shade 411 Driftwood.
  4 (5, 5) x 50g balls (153 yds, 140m per ball).

1 pair size 2 (3mm) needles.

Stitch holder.

Optional: 2.2 yds (2m) fine silk ribbon.

GAUGE
28 sts and 38 rows = 4 x 4" (10 x 10cm) over
  stockinette stitch using size 2 (3mm) needles, or
  needles required to obtain this gauge.

SIZES		
SMALL	MEDIUM	LARGE
To fit bust		
32" (81cm)	34" (86cm)	36" (91.5cm)
Actual size		
32" (81cm)	34½" (87cm)	36½" (93cm)
Bra length		
5½" (14cm)	6" (15cm)	6½" (16.5cm)

GARMENT SIZING See page 124
ABBREVIATIONS See page 126

PATTERN
BACK
Cast on 115 (123, 131) sts.
Knit 4 rows.
Change to St st and cont until
work measures 8¾" (22cm),
ending with a purl row.

Lace panel
Row 1 (RS) K1, p1, k1, *p1, yo,
s1, k2tog, psso, yo, (p1, k1)
twice, repeat from * to end.
Row 2 P1, k1, p1, *k1, p3, (k1,
p1) twice, repeat from * to end.
Rows 3–6 Work as rows 1 and
2 twice. **

Change to St st and work 40 (44,
48) rows.
Change to garter stitch and work
5 rows.
Bind off knitwise.

FRONT

Work as back to **.
Cont as folls.

Row 1 (RS) Knit.

Row 2 P82 (88, 93), k5, turn and work on these sts. Leave rem 28 (30, 33) sts on holder.

Row 3 K7, s1, k1, psso, knit to end – 86 (92, 97) sts.

Row 4 Purl to last 9 sts, p2tog tbl, p2, k5 – 85 (91, 96) sts.

Row 5 Work as row 3 – 84 (90, 95) sts.

Row 6 Purl to last 5 sts, k5.

Rep rows 3–6 until 69 (72, 74) sts rem.

Rep rows 5 and 6 until 62 (65, 67) sts rem, then work row 5 again – 61 (64, 66) sts.

Next row (WS) K8 (11, 13), purl to last 5 sts, k5.

SMALL SIZE ONLY

Row 1 (RS) K7, s1, k1, psso, knit to end – 60 sts.

Row 2 K9, purl to last 9 sts, p2tog tbl, p2, k5 – 59 sts.

Row 3 Work as row 1 – 58 sts.

Row 4 Bind off 5 sts knitwise, k5, purl to last 5 sts, k5 – 53 sts.

Row 5 K7, s1, k1, psso, knit to last 9 sts, k2tog, k7 – 51 sts.

Row 6 K5, purl to last 9 sts, p2tog tbl, p2, k5 – 50 sts.

Row 7 Work as row 5 – 48 sts.

Row 8 K5, purl to last 5 sts, k5.

Rep rows 5 to 8 until 18 sts rem.

Shape top of bra

Row 1 (RS) k7, s1, k1, psso, k2tog, k7 – 16 sts.

Row 2 K5, p2, p2tog tbl, p2, k5 – 15 sts.

Row 3 K7, s1, k2tog, psso, k5 – 13 sts.

Row 4 K5, p3, k5.

*** **Row 5** K5, s1, k2tog, psso, k5 – 11 sts.

Row 6 Knit.

Row 7 K5, s1, k2tog, psso, k3 – 9 sts.

Row 8 Knit,

Row 9 K5, s1, k2tog, psso, k1 – 7 sts.

Row 10 K2tog, k5 – 6 sts.

On 6 sts, work 16½" (42cm) in garter stitch.

Bind off. ***

MEDIUM AND LARGE SIZES

Row 1 (RS) K7, s1, k1, psso, knit to end – 63 (65) sts.

Row 2 K12 (14), purl to last 5 sts, k5.

Row 3 Work as row 1 – 62 (64) sts.

Row 4 Bind off 8 (10) sts knitwise, k5, purl to last 5 sts, k5 – 54 (54) sts.

Row 5 K7, s1, k1, psso, knit to last 9 sts, k2tog, k7 – 52 (52) sts.

Row 6 K5, purl to last 5 sts, k5.

Rep rows 5 and 6 until 46 (34) sts rem.

Cont as folls.

Row 1 K7, s1, k1, psso, knit to last 9 sts, k2tog, k7 – 44 (32) sts.

Row 2 K5, purl to last 9 sts, p2tog tbl, p2, k5 – 43 (31) sts.

Row 3 Work as row 1 – 41 (29) sts.

Row 4 K5, purl to last 5 sts, k5.

Rep rows 1–4 until 21 (29) sts rem.

Cont as folls.

Row 1 K7, s1, k1, psso, knit to last 9 sts, k2tog, k7 – 19 (27) sts.

Row 2 K5, purl to last 9 sts, p2tog tbl, p2, k5 – 18 (26) sts.

Row 3 K7, s1, k1, psso, knit to end – 17 (25) sts.

Row 4 K5, purl to last 5 sts, k5.

LARGE SIZE ONLY
Repeat rows 1–4 until 17 sts rem.

MEDIUM AND LARGE SIZES
Shape top of bra
Row 1 K7, s1, k2tog, psso, knit to end – 15 (15) sts.
Row 2 K5, p1, p2tog tbl, p2, k5 – 14 (14) sts.
Row 3 K7, s1, k1, psso, k5 – 13 (13) sts.
Row 4 K5, p3, k5.
Work *** to *** as on small size shaping.

ALL SIZES
Work second side of bra.
Cast on 59 (63, 65) sts.
Purl across 59 (63, 65) sts, then, with WS facing, purl across 28 (30, 33) sts on holder – 87 (93, 98) sts.
Work to match first side, reversing shaping and noting,
Row 3 Knit to last 9 sts, k2tog, k7.
Row 4 K5, p2, p2tog, purl to end.

FINISHING
Weave in any loose ends. Join side seams. Attach straps to back. Press lightly using a warm iron over a damp cloth.
Optional: Thread the length of silk ribbon through the lace paneling (*see photograph*).

rib and lace cardigan

This slim and stylish lace cardigan is worked in the *finest mercerized cotton*—ideal for cool summer evenings.

MATERIALS

Jaeger Siena 4 ply. Shade 402 Stone.
  10 (11) x 50g balls (153 yds, 140m
  per ball).

1 pair size 2 (3mm) needles.

8 buttons.

2.2 yds (2m) ribbon.

GAUGE

16 sts (2 repeats of lace patt 2) = 2¼"
(6cm) wide after pressing using size 2
(3mm) needles, or needles required to
obtain this gauge.

SIZES	
SMALL–MEDIUM	MEDIUM–LARGE
To fit bust	
32–34" (81–86cm)	36–38" (91.5–96.5cm)
Actual size	
36" (91.5cm)	40" (102cm)
Back length	
22" (56cm)	23" (58.5cm)
Sleeve seam	
19" (48cm)	19" (48cm)

GARMENT SIZING See page 124
ABBREVIATIONS See page 126

PATTERN
BACK

Cast on 126 (142) sts.
Work in lace patt 1 as folls.
Row 1 K3, *yo, s1, k1, psso, k2, repeat from
* to last 3 sts, yo, s1, k1, psso, k1.
Row 2 P3, *yo, p2tog, p2, repeat from * to
last 3 sts, yo, p2tog, p1.
These 2 rows form lace patt 1.
Cont in patt until work measures 5" (12cm).

Change to lace patt 2 as folls.
Row 1 *K3, yo, s1, k1, psso, k1, p2, repeat
from * to last 6 sts, k3, yo, s1, k1, psso, k1.
Row 2 *P3, yo, p2tog, p1, k2 repeat from *
to last 6 sts, p3, yo, p2tog, p1.
These 2 rows form lace patt 2.
Cont in patt until work measures 13" (33cm),
ending with a row 2.

Shape armhole

Bind off 4 (5) sts beg next 2 rows – 118 (132) sts.
Dec 1 st at each end of next and every other row
until 110 (122) sts rem.
Cont without shaping until work measures 21 (21½)"
[53 (55)cm].

Shape shoulders and neck

Bind off 6 sts beg next 6 rows – 74 (86) sts.
Bind off 5 (7) sts beg next 4 rows – 54 (58) sts.
Bind off.

LEFT FRONT

Cast on 70 (78) sts.
Work 5" (13cm) in lace patt 1 as for back.
Change to lace patt 2 and cont until work measures
13" (33cm), ending with a row 2.

Shape armhole

Bind off 4 (5) sts at beg of next row – 66 (73) sts.
Work 1 row.
Dec 1 st at beg next and every other row to 62
(68) sts.
Cont without shaping until work measures 16½"
(42cm), ending with row 1.

Shape neck

Bind off 16 (20) sts at beg of next row – 46 (48) sts.
Dec 1 st at neck edge on next 9 (7) rows – 37
(41) sts.
Dec 1 st at neck edge on next and every other row
until 28 (32) sts rem.
Cont without shaping until work measures same as
back at shoulder, ending with row 2.

Shape shoulder

Bind off 6 sts at beg of next and foll 2 RS rows –
10 (14) sts.
Work 1 row.
Bind off 5 (7) sts beg next row – 5 (7) sts.
Work 1 row.
Bind off.

RIGHT FRONT

Work to match left front reversing all shaping.

SLEEVES

Cast on 70 (70) sts.
Work 1" (2.5cm) in lace patt 1 as on back.

Change to lace patt 2.
Inc 1 st at each end of row 15 and every foll 20th
(10th) row to 80 (92) sts, working extra sts into patt.
Cont without shaping until work measures 19"
(48cm).

Shape sleeve cap

Bind off 4 (5) sts beg next 2 rows – 72 (82) sts.
Dec 1 st at each end of next and every other row
to 40 sts.
Dec 1 st at each end of next 4 rows – 32 sts.
Bind off.

NECKBAND

Join shoulder seams. With RS facing, pick up and knit
50 (54) sts from right front neck, 54 (58) sts from
back neck and 50 (54) sts from left front neck –
154 (166) sts.
Knit 4 rows.
Bind off.

FINISHING

Block pieces to size. Weave in any loose ends. Join
side and sleeve seams. Ease sleeve cap into armhole
and stitch. Sew buttons evenly spaced on lace patt
2, using eyelets for buttonholes. Press lightly using
a warm iron over a damp cloth. Thread the ribbon
through the garment around the waist where lace patt
1 changes to lace patt 2.

boat-neck sweater

Simple shaping creates an elegant silhouette for this chic draped-neck sweater, worked in a beautiful *mercerized cotton.*

MATERIALS
Jaeger Siena 4 ply. Shade 401 White.
  15 (15, 16, 16, 16) x 50g balls
  (153 yds, 140m per ball).

1 pair size 2 (3mm) needles.

1 size 2 (3mm) circular needle.

Stitch holders.

GAUGE
28 sts and 38 rows = 4 x 4" (10 x 10cm) over
  stockinette stitch using size 2 (3mm) needles, or
  needles required to obtain this gauge.

PATTERN
BACK
Cast on 135 (147, 157, 167, 177) sts.
Work in St st, dec 1 st at each end of row 15 and every
foll 20th row until 125 (137, 147, 157, 167) sts rem.
Dec row K3, s1, k1, psso, knit to last 5 sts, k2tog, k3.
Cont without shaping until work measures 16" (40cm).

SIZES				
SMALL	SMALL–MEDIUM	MEDIUM	MEDIUM–LARGE	LARGE
To fit bust				
32" (81cm)	34" (86cm)	36" (91.5cm)	38–42" (96.5cm–107cm)	42–44" (107–112cm)
Actual size				
35" (89cm)	38" (96.5cm)	41" (104cm)	44" (112cm)	47" (119.5cm)
Back length				
22" (56cm)	22½" (57cm)	23" (58.5cm)	23½" (60cm)	24" (61cm)
Sleeve seam				
19" (48cm)	19" (48cm)	19" (48cm)	19" (48cm)	19" (48cm)

GARMENT SIZING See page 124
ABBREVIATIONS See page 126

Shape raglan armhole

Rows 1 and 2 Bind off 5 (7, 9, 11, 13) sts, work to end – 115 (123, 129, 135, 141) sts.

Row 3 K2, s1, k3, psso, knit to end – 114 (122, 128, 134, 140) sts.

Row 4 P2, s1, p3, psso, purl to end – 113 (121, 127, 133, 139) sts.

ALL SIZES EXCEPT SMALL
Repeat rows 3 and 4 until (115, 121, 127, 133) sts rem.

ALL SIZES
* Work 4 rows in St st – 113 (115, 121, 127, 133) sts.
Work rows 3 and 4 again.*
Rep from * to * until 95 (97, 103, 107, 113) sts rem.
Leave sts on holder.

FRONT

Work as for back.

SLEEVES

Cast on 66 (70, 70, 72, 72) sts.

Work in St st, inc 1 st at each end of row 15 and every foll 12th (10th, 8th, 6th, 6th) row to 88 (96, 100, 112, 116) sts.

Cont without shaping until work measures 19" (48cm).

Shape raglan armhole

Rows 1 and 2 Bind off 5 (7, 9, 11, 13) sts, work to end – 78 (82, 82, 90, 90) sts.

Row 3 K2, s1, k3, psso, knit to end.

Row 4 P2, s1, p3, psso, purl to end.

Rep rows 3 and 4 until 22 (20, 20, 22, 22) sts rem.
Leave sts on holder.

COLLAR

Join raglan seams.

With RS facing and using circular needle, work 10" (25cm) in k3, p3 rib across the 234 (234, 246, 258, 270) sts on holders.

Every round *K3, p3, repeat from * to end.
Bind off loosely in rib.

FINISHING

Weave in any loose ends. Join side and sleeve seams. Press lightly using a warm iron over a damp cloth.

lace-sleeved top

This sweet slubbed *silk and cotton* blend top is set off with stylish shaping and lovely lace stitch cap sleeves.

MATERIALS

Jaeger Trinity. Shade 444 Sky.
4 (4, 5) x 50g balls (218 yds, 200m per ball).

1 pair size 3 (3.25mm) and 1 pair size 6 (4mm) needles

Stitch holders.

GAUGE

22 sts and 30 rows = 4 x 4" (10 x 10cm) over stockinette stitch using size 6 (4mm) needles, or needles required to obtain this gauge.

PATTERN

BACK

Cast on 94 (102, 110) sts using smaller needles.
Work ¾" (1.5cm) in k1, p1 rib.

Change to larger needles and St st. Cont until work measures 12 (12¼, 12½)" [31 (31.5, 32)cm].

Shape armholes

Rows 1 and 2 Bind off 3 (4, 5) sts, work to end – 88 (94, 100) sts.
Row 3 K2, p1, s1, k1, psso, knit to last 5 sts, k2tog, p1, k2 – 86 (92, 98) sts.
Row 4 P2, k1, purl to last 3 sts, k1, p2.
Repeat rows 3 and 4 until 72 (72, 74) sts rem.
Dec as established on next and every foll 4th row until 56 (58, 60) sts rem.
Work 3 rows without shaping.
Leave sts on holder.

SIZES		
SMALL	MEDIUM	LARGE
To fit bust		
32" (81cm)	34" (86cm)	36" (91.5cm)
Actual size		
33" (84cm)	36½" (93cm)	39" (99cm)
Back length		
18½" (47cm)	18¾" (47.5cm)	19" (48cm)
Sleeve seam		
¾" (1.5cm)	¾" (1.5cm)	¾" (1.5cm)

GARMENT SIZING See page 124
ABBREVIATIONS See page 126

FRONT

Work as for back.

SLEEVES

Cast on 62 (66, 70) sts using smaller needles.
Work ¾" (1.5cm) in k1, p1 rib.

Change to larger needles and lace patt, and shape
sleeve cap.

Shape sleeve cap

Row 1 Bind off 3 (4, 5) sts, k1 (2, 3) including st
already on RH needle after bind off, *k2tog, yo, k1,
yo, s1, k1, psso, k2, repeat from * to last 2 (4, 6)
sts, k2 (4, 6).
Row 2 Bind off 3 (4, 5) sts, purl to end.
Row 3 K2tog, k3 (4, 5), *yo, s1, k1, psso, k2tog,
yo, k3, repeat from * to last 2 (3, 4) sts, k0 (1, 2),
k2tog.
Rows 4, 6, and 8 Purl.
Row 5 K2tog, k1 (2, 3), *yo, s1, k1, psso, k2,
k2tog, yo, k1, repeat from * to last 2 (3, 4) sts,
k0 (1, 2), k2tog.
Row 7 K2tog, k1 (2, 3), *yo, s1, k1, psso, k2tog,
yo, k3, repeat from * to last 7 (8, 9) sts, yo, s1, k1,
psso, k2tog, yo, k1 (2, 3), k2tog.
Rows 5–8 within the * form lace patt repeat.
Keeping lace patt correct, dec 1 st at each end of
every foll RS row until 40 (44, 48) sts rem, then dec
1 st at each end of every foll 4th row until 26 (28,
30) sts rem.
Work 1 row.
Leave sts on holder.

NECKBAND

Join sleeves to front and right sleeve to back.
With RS facing and using smaller needles, knit across
26 (28, 30) sts of left sleeve, 56 (58, 60) sts of
front, 26 (28, 30) sts of right sleeve, and 56 (58,
60) sts of back – 164 (172, 180) sts.
Work ¾" (1.5cm) in k1, p1 rib.
Bind off in rib.

FINISHING

Weave in any loose ends. Join last raglan seam and
neckband. Join side and sleeve seams. Press lightly
using a warm iron over a damp cloth.

finishing touches

It is important to take time with finishing details. All too often a beautifully knitted garment can be spoiled by rushing the final assembly process. In order to produce a professional finish, it is vital to use the correct method to sew up the seams, and also to pick up borders and neckbands evenly.

Before assembly, weave in all the yarn ends carefully. Press all the knitted pieces, taking care to measure and pin each section so that you do not pull the knitting into a shape that is too wide, too long, or uneven. Always press on the wrong side of the knitted fabric, and use a steam iron or press with a dry iron over a damp cloth to avoid damaging the knitted surface.

Join up each section of knitting in turn, matching rows and taking time to line up pieces accurately. Seams should be as unobtrusive and as neat as possible. There are a number of basic techniques for seaming and assembly. By following these instructions, you will be able to perfect the finishing touches you need for creating extra special luxury pieces.

INVISIBLE SEAM/MATTRESS STITCH

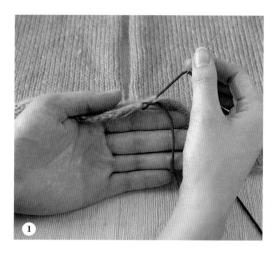

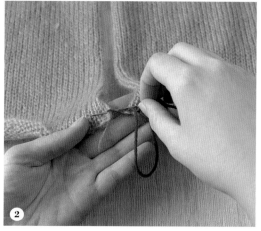

It is important to get a neat edge when joining seams. To achieve this, lay both pieces flat with the right side of the knitting facing upwards and side edges vertical to each other. Thread a sewing needle with yarn and bring it up from the back of the piece on the right as close to the bottom edge and side as possible.

Take the needle across and under the left piece of fabric. Bring it through the left piece from back to front, and back under the right and through to the front, creating a figure eight. This gives a neat start to the seam.

From the front, insert the needle into the side of the next stitch on the piece on the right. Then, pointing the needle up, bring it through to the front, so that two bars of yarn lie across the needle. Pull the needle through.

Take the needle across to the left piece and insert it into the stitch that the last stitch came from. Then, pointing the needle up, bring it through to the front, so that two bars of yarn lie across the needle. Pull the needle through. Continue to work from side to side pulling up the stitches every inch (2cm) to tighten the seam.

JOINING THE SLEEVE TO THE BODY WITH A MATTRESS STITCH

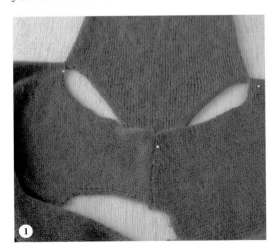

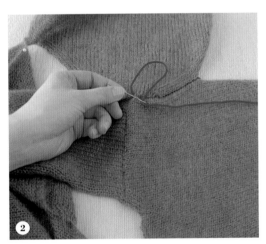

When joining the sleeve to the body, mark the center of the sleeve cap with a pin and match it to the shoulder seam. Secure this center point with a basting stitch (or pin if you prefer). Do the same at the points where the sleeve meets the side edge of the armhole. This will help you to judge the placement of the sleeve cap when you sew the pieces together.

Following the instructions for mattress stitch, stitch the seam, taking one knitted stitch into the seam on the body and stitching as close as possible to the bound-off edge on the sleeve. Bring the sewing needle through the center of the bound-off edge stitch on the sleeve. From the front, insert the needle in between two knitted stitches on the body and bring it through to the front of the work two bars up.

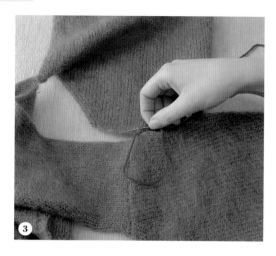

From the front, insert the sewing needle back into the stitch on the sleeve from where the yarn started. Keeping the needle horizontal, bring it through the work two bars along to the left.

Continue to work in this way, but take three bars from the body every couple of stitches. This will ensure that the body and sleeve fit together evenly without stretching.

JOINING SHOULDER SEAMS

On the shoulder seam of a stockinette-stitch garment, you can create an almost invisible seam by using a slight variation of mattress stitch.

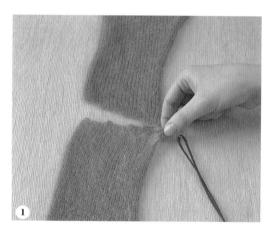

Place the bound-off edges next to each other, one above the other, with the right side of each knitted piece facing upward. Thread a sewing needle with yarn and work from right to left. From the back of the lower piece of knitted fabric, bring the needle up through the first knitted stitch to the front.

From the front, put the sewing needle through the side of the corresponding stitch on the upper piece of knitted fabric. Bring the needle back through to the front, one stitch along to the left.

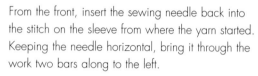

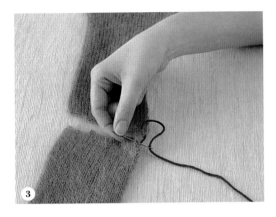

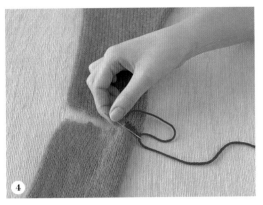

From the front, thread the needle back through the center of the first stitch on the lower piece of fabric where the yarn leaves, then out of the center of the next stitch on the left.

Continue to work along the row, making sure the sewn stitches are the same gauge and size as each other to match the stitches in the knitted rows.

PICKING UP STITCHES

Most knitted pieces have an edging or border of some kind to neaten the raw edge or create a finishing detail. It is important to pick up stitches evenly, particularly around a neckline as this is often the focal point of a garment. The patterns in this book break down the number of stitches that must be picked up along each section of the neck to give an even finish.

PICKING UP STITCHES ALONG A HORIZONTAL EDGE

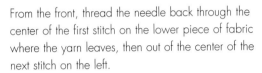

Use one knitting needle and have the right side of the work facing you. Holding the needle in your right hand, insert it through the center of the first stitch from front to back.

Wrap a new piece of yarn around the knitting needle from back to front, as if to knit.

Pull the loop through the knitted stitch to the front.

PICKING UP STITCHES ON A VERTICAL EDGE

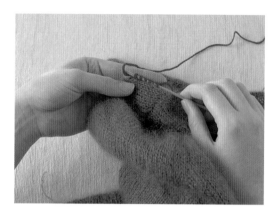

When picking up stitches on a vertical edge, such as down the front, or the back of the neck, use this same method but pick up one stitch in from the edge of the work. Depending on the pattern instructions, not every stitch will be required, so pick up stitches as evenly as possible to avoid stretching certain areas.

PICKING UP STITCHES ALONG A SHAPED EDGE

When picking up stitches around a shaped edge, such as a neckline, pick up one knitted stitch in from the edge to avoid jagged or untidy shaping. When picking up between the knitted piece and any areas that have been left on a stitch holder, be careful not to pick up into the center of any obvious holes.

ATTACHING COLLARS

Collars can be attached to a garment either by picking up stitches or by sewing on after the garment is completed. If a neckline is open, the seam must be as neat as possible as both sides of it will be seen.

To attach a collar evenly, fold it in half or count the knitted stitches to find the center. Join this point to the center back neck with either a pin or a basting stitch. Repeat this with the front edges at each side. Thread a sewing needle with enough yarn to sew the whole seam.

Starting at the center back, bring half the length of yarn through and begin to sew the collar to the neck using a slip stitch or mattress stitch. When the center front is reached, secure the yarn on the inside edge. Return to the center back to stitch the remaining side.

ATTACHING BANDS

Bands are added to garments to flatten and neaten the raw knitted edges. They are often used to add definition or design detail as well as to strengthen and determine the area where the garment is to be fastened. Therefore, a neat and professional finish is very important. It is preferable to use a stitch that creates a narrow seam and one that allows the knitting to be matched as evenly as possible.

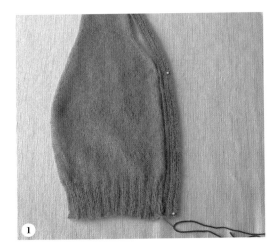

Lay the band and the knitted piece to which it is to be attached side by side, stretching the band very slightly. Pin the band along the front edge of the garment so that the band remains taut and in place when working. Thread a sewing needle with yarn and begin the seam using a mattress stitch.

Take the needle across to the left piece and insert it into the stitch that the last stitch came from. Then, pointing the needle up, bring it through to the front two stitches up. Pull the needle through.

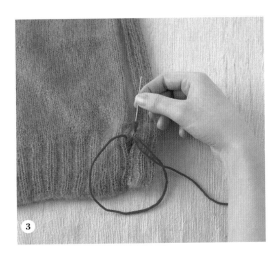

Continue to work from side to side pulling up the stitches every inch (2cm) to tighten the seam. When the top of the band is level with the top of the garment front, bind off or leave on a stitch holder depending on the pattern directions.

garment sizing

The size of a garment is very much a matter of personal taste. Some people prefer a garment to fit snugly while others prefer a larger size for ease and comfort. In general, the patterns in this book err on the generous side for the feeling of relaxation and luxury. The shape of the neckline, the style of the armhole, and the length of the garment can also affect the size you choose to knit. The following sketches of the proportions and general measurements of each design should help you establish which size you prefer to make.

In each pattern, instructions for more than one size are listed smallest first, with the larger sizes listed within parentheses in order of increasing size. It can often be useful to highlight the size you need throughout the pattern instructions to prevent any confusion when knitting.

BABY SWEATER, PAGE 32

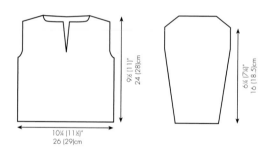

9½ (11)"
24 (28)cm

6¼ (7¼)"
16 (18.5)cm

10¼ (11½)"
26 (29)cm

V-NECK SWEATER, PAGE 42

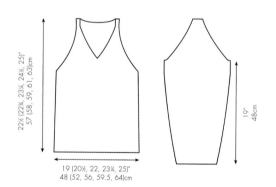

22½ (22¾, 23¼, 24¼, 25)"
57 (58, 59, 61, 63)cm

19"
48cm

19 (20½, 22, 23¼, 25)"
48 (52, 56, 59.5, 64)cm

WRAPAROUND CARDIGAN, PAGE 46

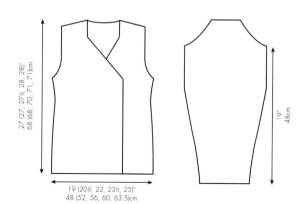

27 (27, 27½, 28, 28)"
68 (68, 70, 71, 71)cm

19"
48cm

19 (20½, 22, 23½, 25)"
48 (52, 56, 60, 63.5)cm

TRAVELING STITCH AND RIB CARDIGAN, PAGE 52

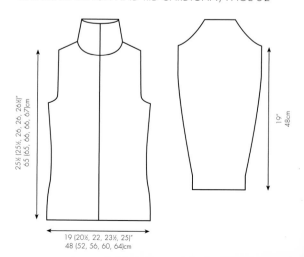

25½ (25¾, 26, 26, 26½)"
65 (65, 66, 66, 67)cm

19"
48cm

19 (20½, 22, 23½, 25)"
48 (52, 56, 60, 64)cm

LACE SWEATER, PAGE 58

22½ (23, 24)"
57 (58.5, 61)cm

18½ (21½, 24½)"
47 (55, 62)cm

19"
48cm

SHAWL COLLAR JACKET, PAGE 62

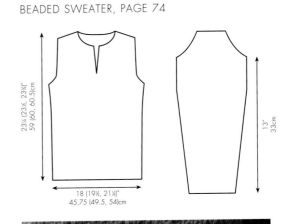

25 (25, 26, 26½, 27)"
64 (64, 66, 67, 68)cm

19½ (21¼, 22¾, 24, 25½)"
49.5 (54, 58, 61, 65)cm

19"
48cm

CROSSOVER CARDIGAN, PAGE 70

19½ (20, 20½)"
50 (51, 52)cm

18 (18½, 20)"
45.75 (47, 51)cm

19"
48cm

BEADED SWEATER, PAGE 74

23¼ (23½, 23¾)"
59 (60, 60.5)cm

18 (19½, 21¼)"
45.75 (49.5, 54)cm

13"
33cm

WIDE-NECK SWEATER, PAGE 80

21½ (22, 22½, 22¾, 23½)"
55 (56, 57, 58, 60)cm

17½ (19¾, 21, 22¾, 24½)"
44.5 (49, 53.5, 58, 62)cm

19"
48cm

BEADED BOLERO, PAGE 84

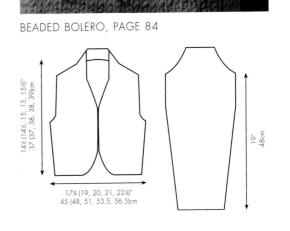

14½ (14½, 15, 15, 15½)"
37 (37, 38, 38, 39)cm

17¾ (19, 20, 21, 22¼)"
45 (48, 51, 53.5, 56.5)cm

19"
48cm

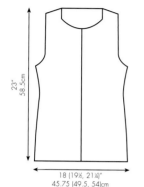

LACE CARDIGAN AND CAMISOLE, PAGE 90

23"
58.5cm

19"
48cm

23"
58.5cm

18 (19½, 21¼)"
45.75 (49.5, 54)cm

16½ (17½, 19½)"
42 (44.5, 49.5)cm

SCOOP-NECK SWEATER, PAGE 98

23½ (23¾, 24, 24½)"
60 (60.5, 61, 62)cm

18½"
47cm

20½ (22, 23½, 25)"
52 (56, 60, 63.5)cm

CAMISOLE, PAGE 102

5½ (6, 6½)"
14 (15, 16.5)cm

16 (17¼, 18¼)"
40.5 (43.5, 46)cm

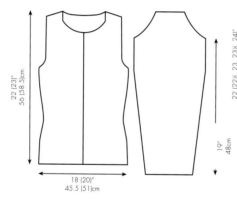

RIB AND LACE CARDIGAN, PAGE 106

22 (23)"
56 (58.5)cm

19"
48cm

18 (20)"
45.5 (51)cm

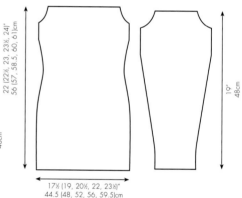

BOAT-NECK SWEATER, PAGE 110

22 (22½, 23, 23½, 24)"
56 (57, 58.5, 60, 61)cm

19"
48cm

17½ (19, 20½, 22, 23½)"
44.5 (48, 52, 56, 59.5)cm

LACE-SLEEVED TOP, PAGE 114

18½ (18¾, 19)"
47 (47.5, 48)cm

16½ (17¾, 19)"
42 (45, 48)cm

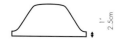

1"
2.5cm

List of Abbreviations

" = inch(es)

approx. = approximately

cm = centimeters

cont = continue

dec = decrease

foll = following

inc = increase

k = knit

k2tog = knit the next 2 sts together

k2togb = knit the next 2 sts together through the back loops

m = meters

mm = millimeters

p = purl

p2tog = purl next 2 stitches together

p2togb = purl next 2 stitches together through the back loops

patt = pattern

psso = pass the slipped stitch over

rem = remain(ing)

RS = right side

s1 = slip the next stitch

st(s) = stitch(es)

St st = stockinette stitch

tbl = through back loop

WS = wrong side

wyib = with yarn in back

wyif = with yarn in front

yds = yards

yo = yarn over needle from purl position to knit position to make a stitch, or yarn under then over needle from knit to knit or purl to purl position to make a stitch

index

suppliers and acknowledgments

Yarn suppliers

Debbie Bliss yarns

For further information visit the Debbie Bliss website:
www.debbieblissonline.com

Australia
Jo Sharp Pty Ltd
ACN 056 596 439
PO Box 1018
Fremantle WA 6959
Tel: (08) 9430 9699
Email: yarn@josharp.com.au
www.josharp.com.au

Canada
Diamond Yarn
9697 St Laurent
Montreal
Quebec H3L 2N1
Tel: (514) 388 6188

Diamond Yarn
155 Martin Ross, Unit 3
Toronto
Ontario M3J 2L9
Tel: (416) 736 6111
Email: diamond@diamondyarn.com
www.diamondyarns.com

U.K.
Designer Yarns Ltd
Units 8–10 Newbridge Industrial Estate
Pitt Street
Keighley
West Yorkshire BD21 4PQ
Tel: (01535) 664222
Email: jane@designeryarns.uk.com
www.designeryarns.uk.com

U.S.A.
Knitting Fever Inc. and Euro Yarns
35 Debevoise Avenue
Roosevelt
New York 11575

Tel: (516) 546 3600
Email: knittingfever@knittingfever.com
www.knittingfever.com

Jaeger yarns

See the supplier details for Jaeger's parent company, Rowan.

Rowan yarns

For further information call Rowan Yarns direct on: +44 (0)1484 681 881 or visit their website: www.knitrowan.com

Australia
Australian Country Spinners
314 Albert Street
Brunswick
Victoria 3056
Tel: (03) 9380 3888

Canada
Diamond Yarn
9697 St Laurent
Montreal
Quebec H3L 2N1
Tel: (514) 388 6188

Diamond Yarn
155 Martin Ross, Unit 3
Toronto
Ontario M3J 2L9
Tel: (416) 736 6111
Email: diamond@diamondyarn.com
www.diamondyarn.com

New Zealand
Alterknitives
PO Box 47961
Auckland
Tel: (09) 376 0337

Knitworld
Shop 210b, Cuba Mall
Wellington
Tel: (04) 385 1918

U.K.
Rowan
Green Lane Mill
Holmfirth
West Yorkshire HD9 2DX
Tel: (01484) 681881

U.S.A.
Rowan USA
4 Townsend West, Suite 8
Nashua
New Hampshire 03063
Tel: (603) 886 5041/5043
Email: wfibers@aol.com

RY Classic yarns

See the supplier details for Rowan.

Acknowledgments

The author would like to thank family and friends for their support, especially Jeff and Eve. Many thanks to Eva Yates for her hours of hard work, lovely phone calls, and knitting wisdom; Gill Everett for all her help and her fantastic team of knitters; Kate Buller for the kind sponsorship of Rowan and Jaeger yarns; and Ann Hinchcliffe for all her help. Thanks also to Jane at Designer Yarns for supplying the lovely Debbie Bliss yarns, the models, Krissy and Tashi, at Jackie Jones model agency, Jackie Jones for hair and makeup, and Kate Kirby, Jo Fisher, Anna Knight, and all at Quarto who have helped in realizing this book.